FREELANCER

A NOVEL

———————

CRISTIAN S. ALUAŞ

Freelancer

Paperback ISBN: 978-0-9877981-3-8

Masterpiece Art School LLC

www.masterpieceartschool.com

DEDICATION

To the Dumas: Veronica, *Reghina*, and Teodor

freelancer <u>noun</u>

free·lanc·er | \ ˈfrē-ˌlan(t)-sər\

plural freelancers

Definition of freelancer

1

: a person who pursues a profession without a long-term commitment to any one employer, often an artist

Overnight, I had a dream about the best kind of love. In the dream, I was with a lover. She had plump cheeks and a tender way about her. We were embracing.

Looking in her colourless eyes, I had a vision. I told her, "The forest in the daytime is not as scary as the nighttime."

That was my revelation.

"In relationships, we should always show ourselves in the best light, especially at the beginning," I told her. "The forest must first be trekked in the daytime, so the terrain becomes familiar. That way, when the hours are late, it will never get as *dark* because we know the territory very well. We know the territory very well *in the best light*. We never need to go to those dark places because those dark places don't exist to us anymore. Everything is lit because we know it from the best light. We don't get scared. We don't get lost. We see even the darkest things about ourselves in the best light. Therefore, that makes for *the best kind of love*."

When I finished with my proclamation, we kissed. She realized I accepted her. What she saw in herself as her darkest secrets didn't scare me. We had already touched on those dark subjects, lightly, when outside was bright.

. . .

I met Emily at a coffee shop in the Glebe. She was a barista. We had nothing in common, except our mutual attraction to each other. I flamed her vanity with compliments each time I saw her, and then I asked if she'd like to come and see my drawings. At one point, she told me she was living with a dude. But she came anyway. Her clothes slipped to the floor within minutes. She stood there nude and vulnerable. Goosebumps on her arms and my neck.

My free-spirited barista had a red birthmark the size of a one dollar coin on her shoulder. She hid it with a rose tattoo. Most people would never know, except she couldn't help herself to always mention it. Her blonde hair was long enough to cover it. She posed with her other shoulder toward me, hiding her rose-coloured mark. Her equine nose reflected the light in a way that directed everything to her eyes. Her bedroom lids relaxed over perfectly clear marbles. The colour of them rainbow. The unwrinkled bowls which held her eyes rested on sharp cheekbones. The double light, like tears along her jawline, framed her thin balmed lips.

I was in the zone.

"When I paint someone from life I try to represent their natural beauty. That's the role of a good artist," I told her.

"This is so cool," she said. "You know how to make a girl feel special."

It was first in high school where I learned to draw the model. Having attended an arts academy, life drawing was part of the application process. I also had figure drawing classes in college, and I remember some of the students would giggle or become shy. That never happened to me. I could look at a nude objectively. My cool was always kept. The silence of those classrooms rung true to my calling. My mind relaxed. My fingers tightened around my 2B pencil, and I let nirvana find me. I realized then that life study is the closest thing to Tao that a Western artist has.

Working online as a comic book illustrator wasn't enough. What I really wanted to be was an artist in the grandest sense of the word. Michelangelo, Rembrandt, Picasso; these were the guys I idolized. But I didn't have divine inspiration or famous patrons. All I had was a community college degree and the daily demands of food and rent. I took any graphic design and illustration gigs I could get. In my spare time, I'd drive out to the Nepean Sportsplex where nobody knew me and experiment with watercolour and acrylic paints. It became my habit that even dates were combined into practice.

I painted my barista for a couple hours. The underpainting was a drawing. Then I built up the figure, leaving the background out. The way I approached oil painting was like Rembrandt. Thin and dark to thick and light. Impasto would have been the better method for a quick painting but I went with a style that fit the mood of my studio. The dim-lit room set Emily at ease. And that was worth having a muddy painting. When she asked for a break to stretch her legs, my squinting eyes relaxed.

Emily smoked a cigarette on the balcony, wearing one of my dress shirts. Only two buttons were done up. She stared out toward the townhouses and parking lot to the side. A residential lamplight silhouetted the folds in the shirt, her nose, and her legs. Her gaze was even with the horizon. Her thoughts seemed in a deep conversation with the half-covered moon.

The guy she said she lived with was probably her boyfriend. I didn't ask questions. Having her pose nude for me was an opportunity to get to know her. Perhaps I'd play the long game, in case she wasn't single. I never liked the idea of stealing someone from their boyfriend, ever since I saw a friend do that to someone. Years later she got stolen from him. I believe it was Casanova who said, "Good lovers borrow, while great lovers steal." And bad criminals are always haunted by their conscience. If you live honest, you live modest but you sleep well at night, even if you're alone.

She threw her cigarette over the balcony, and came inside. She asked if she could hop into the shower. Why not? I was cleaning up and putting away my paint supplies, when she called from the steamy doorway. For the first time, she looked at me with sex in her eyes. She was naked with her legs akimbo. There's a thin line between nude and naked, only artists see. A nude body is an objective experience, while a naked body is subjective inside and out.

The way she presented herself to me left our lips with no other subject.

My black two-door coupe rode the waves of the 417 East in fifth gear. Music drummed on the radio. The side of my car was decorated with muddied water from salted roads. At 8AM each Saturday, my trek was predictably 40 minutes, ascending the Ottawa valley into the rising sun.

I came a long way already. My earliest memories were riding in a cart with my grandfather, *from my mother's side*. The steer pulling us. The wheels turning. He was a good honest man. He taught me that, despite good or bad seasons, nothing will grow unless you plant your seeds and toil the land. Every day, you must get up and keep trying. Keep working. And to get to promised places, you sometimes have to whip the steer to keep the wheels rolling.

Ottawa, Ontario, Canada. The nation's capital. It wasn't the ideal place for an artist but anyone would be lucky to have grown up here, with bicycle rides along the Rideau River. But as I advanced in my career, I realized more and more each day that Ottawa wasn't exactly New York or London. A few months ago, I had a band crash in my living room. They drove a used van from Vancouver through the prairies to the East Coast. They played house concerts and any other gigs they could get. I booked them as an opening act for a local band I knew. On the way to the gig, we drove past Sparks Street toward the parliament buildings, one in the passenger seat and three in the back.

The lead singer said, "Nice little town you have here."

Fine little town to grow up in. To raise a family. It was clean and safe. With suburbs like Nepean, Orleans, and Kanata amalgamated into the city sprawl, the total population was barely one million. Out of those, 200,000 worked for the federal government. Tolstoy wrote that all families are the same, each with their own set of problems. The same could be said about towns. The city centers all have the same cuteness, as if their uniqueness was factory-made. The shop-keepers are all welcoming, the business people relatively bustling, and the peddlers at the farmer's markets smiley, all the same.

But once you dove in deeper into any given town, you'd find out its foundation. In Ottawa's case, the government seemed like Atlas holding me trapped in the sphere on its shoulders. One among a million. As an artist, I felt confined to painting with a limited palette. This town wanted me to conform to its uniformity. Much like the design of the Canadian flag. A single coloured Rorschach, framed by barriers on either side.

Like a rock skipping over water, if you don't move you sink. The propulsion of my ambitions, to find love, to find success beyond my boundaries, propelled me forward. The St. Laurent Boulevard exit was upon me and I took it, spritely weaving through industrial then residential streets.

"1365 Bank Street, apartment 1505. 1365 Bank Street, apartment 1505..." He kept repeating my address loudly.

David was the first autistic kid I had in these art classes. Every line he put on paper had no doubts. That's half the artist's battle, to have no insecurity in the brush line. When he became too old for the 6-13 year old classes, I still let his parents sign him up. It was tough for them to find activities for him, especially ones he liked. In the summers, when the community centre didn't run programming, I propped a table in my living room to teach him. He memorized my address. The nerves from the misbehaving boys made him share too much.

The class was out of control.

I knew my material but I still hadn't mastered disciplining children. Drawing examples on the flip chart at the front of the class left chaos behind me. Paint and rubber erasers flew in the air. Two ten year old brothers were the instigators.

The noise went on until I finally burst. I stood up to the ten year old brothers and said, "If you don't stop and listen, I'm gonna throw you out of the class and I'm not gonna open the door... I'm gonna throw you out through the plexiglass window."

Twenty minutes later, I got to hear it from the boys' mother. "Did you threaten my children?"

"Of course not," I said. "I merely told them that I'd put them out of the class if they didn't behave."

"They said you were going to throw them through the window," she said.

"Wow. What an imagination," I told her.

The watercolour teacher overheard me. She came to me after the parent left. "You have to be firm and they listen."

"I think it's 'cause I'm a man," I told the teacher. "There's something about a mother's tone that's not as harsh as a man's."

"Can you grow a decent beard? That might help," she said. "You're too much of a baby face. They walk all over you." She was a quirky lady who made giclée illustrations. "If you grow a beard," she told me, "or better yet goatee, they're going to know you're the grown up."

"I just think I'm ill prepared. I get nervous up there and I get in the habit of drawing examples on the flip chart. Today I was afraid to look behind me. By the time I did, I had enough."

"Print out some instructions. That helps. Hand them out and then supervise. And don't forget the beard."

She left and I went into the office.

In the drawer, I found a Manila folder with my name on it. Today being the last class of the Spring, I was expecting my final paycheck which would help finance part of my summer months until classes started up again in the Fall. I felt my spirits sink when I picked it up and felt it lighter than it should be. I slammed the empty folder onto the abandoned desk. My palm made a bang. Parents turned to look toward me, through the glass partition.

The reason why I chose to be an artist was so I wouldn't depend on any employer. I wanted to work for myself. Here I was, back again, dependent on a damn paycheck.

The Canterbury Community Centre was run by a caring religious couple, Chandri and Gary Frank. The programming was all their initiative but the city of Ottawa owned the sportsplex where the classes were held. This was their pride and joy. In the ten years they ran it, it grew exponentially. They offered art classes and also indoor and outdoor sports classes, Mommy and Me singing classes, swimming, basket weaving, knitting, you name it. As soon as the City saw their volunteer venture was making money, they stepped in and, feeling they could manage it better, pulled the rug from under them. Chandri and Gary were devastated.

When the city took over their programming last Fall, you could see the quality decline everywhere immediately. No more Christmas bonuses, the newsprint course catalogue downgraded in design and paper quality, and now the accounting was behind.

"Hello. This is Alex Emin. The art teacher," I said. My voice cracked with emotion. "I put the invoice in for my services early. Over a month ago. I was assured by you that the cheque would be ready two weeks ago. What can I do to expedite this process, besides begging for what I have rightfully earned?" My tone was what people called passive-aggressive. In polite society, it's considered worse than actual aggression. "If there is anything I can do to help you do your job, please let me know. If I knew accounting, I would happily do your job for you," I added.

The City brought in their own accountant. We were introduced during registration week. He was bloated and middle-aged, drenched with perspiration and smelling of a paper spindle. After his appearance on the scene, the cheques began to come late. He once explained, since the city runs things, there was extra bureaucracy added to the process. One extra person had to sign off on the cheques.

"Please let me know at your earliest convenience when I should come in to pick up my cheque. I now have to travel an extra hour each way, just to pick it up, so please let me know ASAP, so I don't keep wasting my time."

I was overdoing it, I realized too late. Resent is the most unattractive trait, not just in relationships but in business too. Waking up early on Saturdays was a personal sacrifice I made for my career. At least I should get my cheese at the end of the maze, I thought.

I stormed out of the office, down the hallway and out of the building. The afternoon shadows followed me along the pavement to my car.

In the corner of the Centre d'Orleans was an arts organization. When they developed the place, it was likely a quota to add the community component. The Orleans Art League also ran the gallery where local artworks were juried and exhibited. The look of the sportsplex was like every other. This one was brand new and five times as big as Canterbury, with multiple offices, and a hockey rink.

The Canterbury accountant called back. He said, "Your cheque is ready. I played your call to my supervisors and you're fired."

Now I was here. Looking for another gig.

My high school had the same white walls made out of porous cement. They were the type of industrial walls built to keep thousands of students in and creativity out. The smell of Zambonied ice and chlorine made for fresh cool sterilized breaths. Wind currents flowed around me as I walked past glass trophy cases with awards that were left behind, nobody wanted, and photos of government workers that facilitated the centre's construction. The floors were a janitor's dream. The tapping of my black polished Bostonians echoed through the empty hallways. The shoes were the only dressy ones I had. The grey slacks I was wearing I've had for several years.

They say in Japanese culture, clothes could be possessed by spirits. Clothes possessed me. I had a high respect for how they made me feel. I was always careful with the first experience of each item I wore. To break it in right. To have good memories associated.

When I was in a broke way and starting out with social assistance, I looked for dress pants with my first allowance. With that first cheque, I bought grey dress pants and had the cuffs turned up. The first time I took them out, a splash of paint fell on my knee when I was demonstrating. "You're not an artist, if you don't get dirty," a student used to say.

I strode the sportsplex hallways proudly, wearing speckled survivors from successful campaigns. My white dress shirt and my one and only rust-coloured blazer glided with me around corners like a dry cleaner's conveyer. This wool-blended blazer was bought for my first college interview. We've had great memories since. I wore him carefully, to last. The design was slightly dated, with more padding in the shoulders than the trend now. It was designed for professionals more mature than I. That was my attraction. Its silk interior and the cut were acting as my mentor.

The office number was on a 2x8 inch linoleum plaque screwed into the cement above the door. My tie was Harry Rosen. She was discovered among a hundred others and bought for five bucks from the Salvation Army. I pinched her knot like Rodney Dangerfield, before the heavy door clanked shut behind me. I almost expected to hear a spin release lever from outside the door, closing me inside a bank vault. The drill was clear. In front of her desk was a plastic chair. The orange kind that you see in every school stacked up. My resume slid across her desk and I sat down crossing my arms in my lap.

"I already printed a copy," she said, without a welcoming gest.

My interviewer perused my CV while I tried not to squirm in my seat. I stared around the room listening to the sound of paper being flipped between her fingers. Her nails were manicured, bringing to mind the smell of acetone. My eyes strummed across her desk like dominoes but quicker like piano. I saw a keyboard, monitor, and nothing else. The eagerness to work outweighed all judgements I would've had if we were dating. She must have been only a couple years older than me. Hair tied in a bun. She looked like she exercised.

My eyes shifted to the blank wall behind her and I began to imagine what I might create if I were alone in here with my brushes, paints, and stencils. The colours of the Romanian flag are blue, yellow, and red. The primaries. All other colours can be mixed out of those three. I was made from those three colours. They ran in my blood. Everything I saw, I saw through those colours, like tinted glasses. Rivers of colours flowed between mountains, on the walls around me. Fluorescent drips up close.

"Based on your education and experience, you can only teach illustration to children," she said. Her voice jolted me out of my daydream. She continued. "It says here you applied to teach the adult painting workshop."

Teaching adults instead of children seemed like the next natural stage of my career.

"I paint every day," I told her. "I've been painting and doing shows in cafes and bars and some small galleries for as long as I've been a full-time artist."

"Your resume says you mostly taught children," she said, "and you only have a Diploma in Illustration and an incomplete Bachelors in Fine Art."

"What about my six years experience," I asked her.

Walking in I remembered her name but now, full of emotion, I didn't care. My tone was defensive.

"This is a city organisation, Alex. You need a Masters degree to teach painting." She was clearly using "the city" as a cloak to make her own judgement. At least that's the way I saw it. I blinked hard to rid the red that I saw. "It's not me. It's the city," she said, showing me her palms. I rather preferred she reject me outright, rather than drag me along. "I totally understand," she added. "I'm an artist too. I have a Masters in Fine Art and another in Office Administration. I wouldn't have gotten my position if I didn't have two Masters degrees. It's just the way it is."

Government or corporate, they all had the same army mentality. Rank mattered most. I was coming in cold. Dreams, ambitions, and a colourful palette. I was never going to paint those walls. That, I had to understand.

"Right," was all I could muster.

It wasn't clear what other applicants I was up against but the camp started the following week.

"Go back to school. It's definitely a great option. Upgrade your eligibility," she said.

"I'll consider it. Thanks," I said. But there was no turning back in my mind. I'd come too far. To go back to school would be to admit defeat in the real world.

"So, are you available next week to teach our kids Illustration camp," she asked. I looked up and she had a satisfied look on her face, like she ate a really warm slice of pie. "You're not qualified for the painting course but we need someone to teach illustration." She relished putting me in my place.

She looked at me wanting to see a thankful smile for the favour she did me. I bowed and stretched my arm out for a handshake. The only way to make a living as an artist was to fall in line and turn to the mercy of the dollar. I accepted my position.

Walking past the door chime and the peppy greeting from the nearby cashier, a determined strut propelled me among the aisles. My arm hooked a shopping basket on the way in.

Malick's Art Supplies had four stores in Ottawa. I walked the aisles of the original Bank and Lisgar Street location. The owner was supposedly an artist but his work was never displayed anywhere, not even in the framing section. The stores had been around for twenty years. There were several locations throughout Ontario, with at least two more in Toronto. It was an art supply chain that aimed to become a monopoly. In fact, only about 15 blocks down Bank Street, they ran a smaller shoppe called Art Guise out of business.

The bigger the chain the better the prices. Malick's had their sourcing down pat. They even had their own branded sketchbooks, paint, and canvases at a lower cost than any of the other brands they carried. Even when they were open, it was hard to shop at Art Guise because with a hobby or profession such as art, every penny counted. Throughout an artist's school years and even their professional years, one had to purchase student-quality paints or products. To save a buck, I sometimes bought on clearance, drippy, crusty, oil paint tubes, pencils with broken leads throughout, and cheap plastic-haired brushes.

Dude, a text came in. *How did it go with the barista?*

A gentleman doesn't tell, I texted back.

This time, I wanted to get the best. The client was a blue chip art collector. I met him at the Strathcona Park Art fair last summer. My polite upbringing forced me to address him as Dr. Weissman. He never offered I should call him otherwise.

At the park, he only bought a five dollar greeting card from me. Not wanting to be salesy, I waited patiently all this time. The trick to making an art sale was to make the client ask. I learned this after seeing galleries without price labels next to the pieces. The attendants never approached. They made the patron come to see the catalogue and inquire. In a way, mine was a similar strategy. Getting the call from Dr. Weissman out of the blue was a humbling relief. The money would come at a perfect time, since all I had right now were some online gigs and the Orleans Sportsplex workshop.

Dr. Weissman chose the canvas dimensions and told me I could pick the subject and the price. Dollar signs came to my eyes but I applied restraint when I quoted him. After all, I was not an established artist. I suspected he called me under the advice of his wife who was with him at our first meeting. She wasn't a collector but she dabbled in painting. Contributing a suggestion of whom to collect was a way they could bond. He was used to paying hundreds of thousands of dollars for works. The least he ever paid for dead artists was $10,000 for signed prints.

Some of my works were listed on websites for a mere five hundred to a thousand so I had to keep it around that range, in case he did his research. After a short deliberation, I asked if he agreed $2,500 was fair. He said, "$2,000 is better."

I conceded. He had all the cards. I had no brand.

Haha, my buddy Eric texted. *I got some news to share.*

Cool, I texted back.

Finally, with a high-end client, I could splurge on quality brushes. No more of those cheap ones from the hardware store. First into my basket were some Rafael fine brushes, number two, and a few varying flats, six, eight, and 14. Then I went to the paint aisle. Finer oil paints, some a hundred dollars plus a tube, were in a nearby glass case. I wasn't that ambitious yet, sticking with the 20-40 dollar range. If an artist knew their colour theory, they could mix all the colours they needed from the three primary colours, yellow, red, and blue. Opting for cadmium for the first two, some phthalo blue was thrown in as the third primary. Black I already had plenty of. Behind the glass, I saw a 37ml tube of Flake White oil paint for $45. I called one of the clerks over to open the glass case.

The manager came. He jiggled his keys. I imagined he had a master's degree in Curatorial Studies or something like that. There was little respect in my heart for practical workers. In my teenage years, I applied at all these shops but never even got an interview so I admit some bitterness came from that.

I saw my career as an artist like living in the wild. The manager, the framer, the part-time student cashier, they were all scared little mice warm in the farmer's barn. They just had to do the bare minimum for a little over minimum wage. By the time they were done work, they were too exhausted for anything else. Their creative ambitions put on hold. I wondered if they also resented working artists coming in every day, going about their business.

The manager had low energy. Most of the employees were like that, unless they just got hired. You saw it at all types of jobs. People do shoddy work when they feel it's beneath them so they don't even try to apply themselves. When you think you're a slave, the only motivator is the whip. And the only whip is at the day job. Their art career waned. My struggle seemed worth it, imagining that the Malick's employees sold out.

We still on for tonight, asked Eric through a text.

"Next, please," the cashier waved. "These canvases are an awesome deal," she added, excited, as I placed products on the counter.

"Yeah, sure." I didn't even look at her.

"Are you a teacher," she asked.

"I teach, yeah."

"Great! Can I see your school board ID card?"

I realized now why she asked. Teachers and students got discounts.

"I teach for a community centre," I replied, the words slightly bitter in my mouth. "They don't give out ID cards."

"It's okay," she smiled at me, holding out her hand to pass the items. "I'll put you in the system anyway," she whispered, leaning in with a side hand and a wink.

Watching her fingers return to her monitor, I said, "Thanks." I couldn't tell why she was being so kind.

She asked for a piece of ID with my name and address so I handed her my driver's license. Her eyes travelled from one end of the screen to the other, as her fingers tap-danced on the keyboard. This gave me a pause to glance at her name tag.

"*Effie*. That's very unique," I said.

"It's short for Aphrodite," she grinned. "It's Greek. But my parents are Irish," she laughed.

"Ahh, very interesting."

Just then, Eric came in on a video call.

"Hey, I'll call you back."

"Who's that with you," he asked, "She's cute. Your new girlfriend?"

My cheeks went red and Effie the cashier got timid.

"I'm at the checkout. What's up?"

"Just seeing if we're on for tonight."

"We're on," I said and hung up.

"Working on a show," asked Effie, trying to distract me from the interruption.

"These? Yeah. Well, one's a commission," I replied. "The other one's for me. I don't have a gallery lined up yet, but hopefully soon."

"Cool. I'm an artist too," she said. Up until this point, she had a peppy voice. It dropped, revealing a more human tone.

"Nice," I offered her a real smile, which she returned.

Everything I claimed to hate about these artist sellouts I was willing to toss out the window. I didn't mean all that. The bitter talk was just the envy of an artist having a hard time, justifying his life choices.

For the first time, I noticed her. I really paid attention. A petite girl in her early twenties. Underneath her Malick's smock, she wore a knee-length vintage dress with ruffled shoulders. Fishnet stockings, slightly torn, fleshed out her thighs. She had a very artsy look about her and I could tell it was her actual style and not just art store policy. She was a clear and natural pale of Irish with rose pedal cheeks. No makeup needed. Her hair was green with golden highlights. Her eyes were tall and sparkled blue. I caught myself just watching her eyelashes wave back at me.

I looked her up and down, trying to figure her out. In that moment's fleet, her side of things seemed reasonable to me. She was just a young girl in love with the arts. She wasn't burdened by trying to make a living from her craft. It was comforting enough to just be in the vicinity of other artists, to be helpful, to be inspired. Her voyage seemed uncharted. The present will make its course to future, without push for time. A career in the arts was no ambition for her. Rub some pennies together, buy some hair dye, get some piercings, needle her experiences into her skin with red and blue ink. That'd be lovely and enough for now.

Effie didn't judge me, like I judged her co-workers. She was just here to put me into the system and give me a discount.

"Two hundred and forty-seven dollars and sixty-eight cents. Cash or credit?"

A moment punctured by a sour taste. The bill.

"Credit," I replied, holding out my card.

She swiped it, I paid in silence, and she handed me my art supplies in a plastic bag. The canvases had handles taped to them for easy carrying.

"Don't forget your phone," she said.

My phone was on the counter. I laughed, embarrassed, snatched my phone and bowed.

Walking to the exit, I couldn't help glance back at Effie, and when I did she looked right back at me and waved, "Good luck."

Eric said, "Shut the door."

I slid in after parking my coupe next to his sedan. He extended the weed pipe over to me, holding the smoke in his lungs. It was a special pipe, very ornate, with shaved wood around reflective bronze.

The copper taste from the pipe was as pronounced as the weed. I watched the embers redden just beyond my nose. The neon sign that read "NuDen" glowed on the windshield. Industrial warehouses all around.

"She's 22. Blonde and stacked," he said. "Check this out." He pulled out his phone, scrolling through pictures. The screen displayed a naked woman, with Eric's mouth attached to her breast.

"Jesus. What if I have to meet her?"

"You should. Let's double date," he said.

We went inside.

The music in the club rang in my head. Thoughts fought to clarify themselves, separating lyrics from their rhythm. Fluorescent figures highlighted the backdrop, like dancing shadows onto Plato's cave.

"An old girlfriend once told me that stripping is a choice for liberated women. Do you believe that?"

Eric said, "I believe women do whatever they want in this world, with some physical restrictions."

"All I know is, they make a lot more cash than I do degrading myself as a commercial illustrator. And for a lot fewer hours of work," I said.

"Yeah but you don't have to be standing in heels all night."

Eric sat next to me. He was in his element, pouting with coolness, his elbows sprawled out atop the couch cushions level with his shoulders. We came here almost every week for years. I was the only one that was outgrowing it.

The DJ came through the speakers with a thick radio voice.

Coming to the stage is a rare sparkling gem, he said. *She's priceless, but she does have a price… so make sure to take her for a dance. Put your hands together and have your dollar bills ready for… Diamond!*

People say you should dance like no-one is watching. But if everyone's watching, you should give them a show. After the DJ's announcement, the room filled with wolf-whistles and men's cheers. A regular Tex Avery cartoon come to life. An extremely fit and tall woman walked down the staircase to the stage, her private parts covered by body paint and a vest made of glitter. The song she began to strut to was a rap song with strong bass.

"Hey boys! What'll it be?" The voice stopped me from staring. Our server stood over us in a short skirt and crop top with the first few buttons undone.

"I'll have whatever's on tap," Eric called out, his eyes still stuck on Diamond.

"And you?" The server leaned over. The thick cake on her face hid her acne.

"Bottle of water," I yelled up at her, over the music and hooting. "I'm the designated driver," I had to explain. I always felt cheap ordering water, even though it was only a buck less than beer. The server giggled and walked off.

"Wasn't she cute," asked Eric.

"I guess."

"What's the matter, man," he finally asked, a little mad at me for spoiling his good mood.

I had a feeling in my chest without a definition.

"I was thinking about Jack Kirby," I said.

"Jack who?"

"He was a comic artist. Everybody in comics loved him," I said. "He created Captain America and the Fantastic Four. He had a crazy long career. He worked non-stop for a paycheck."

"That sounds pretty good to me," said Eric.

"You don't understand," I said. "He was chained to his desk. He was a slave in a slave ship. He just learned to live with the stings of the whip on his back. The comic business kept him at his ravaged table. The same one he had throughout his whole career. He never even learned to drive. Why bother, when you're being driven into the ground? It's like that famous cartoon by Robert Crumb. It's a one page thing. Shows a guy being born, a bunch of shit happens, and then he keels over in a grave. End of story."

"That's everybody's life," he said. "What's your point?"

"My point is I want something different. I don't wanna be chained to my desk, Eric. I wanna be mobile."

"I get it. You wanna be the guy administering the whip." He laughed.

"I wanna be recognized," I told him.

"I recognized you as soon as you walked in," he said. "I known you since high school." He was being smart.

"I'm serious, Eric. I want to be recognized for something other than cartoons."

"You just want to be famous."

"I've been at it seven years already. Hustling non-stop," I said.

Eric was getting fed up. He said, "You know what, man, you're being selfish. What do you think I'm doing here? You know, I'm in Graphic Design because of you. I quit working overnight at Zellers, cashed my stock options, and followed you with this thing. Waking up when you want. Charge whatever you want. Be your own boss. If you hate what you do so much, give it up then. Do something else. Go back to school like I did."

"There's no going back for me," I realized. "I'm in too deep," I told him. "The only course I have is to veer off. Take the fork."

Before every rebellion there's always frustration among the people. I knew my anger was my driving force. Eric saw it only as a nuisance.

Our drinks came. The server sensed the mood in the air, took her money, said nothing, and left. Eric took a few big gulps.

I looked around for branches. There were none. Just beams of light on leather-tanned flesh. The music beat on my eardrums, vibrated my skin, and irritated my good taste. The strobe lights shot across the silhouettes on stage. The smell of Canadian beer carried a bitter scent through the air, mixing with fragrant perfumes that competed for attention. A couple tables over, several men were spread out on a black-lit velvet couch. They had bottle service for a bachelor party. Two dancers twerked on the main man, another with her breasts in a lucky guy's face, and the fourth negotiated a price, cheek to ear. Her thick pink lipstick rubbed off slightly on his ear lobe.

"Yeah, you know, I'm sorry," I said. I didn't tell Eric about losing the gig at the Canterbury Community Centre. I didn't want to discourage him, so I left it at that.

He said, "Sell some paintings. You'll be fine." He had no patience.

"Hello boys! Keen I sit," she asked with a Russian accent and bedroom eyes.

"Sure," said Eric, jumping at the chance to change the atmosphere. Her ass was already on the cushion between us, before he finished the syllable.

She wore a black lace camisole that hid nothing, and white shorts with a dark g-string showing through. Her shoulders and back were covered in tattoos, plenty of bracelets and anklets, and a belly button jewel. Her gold necklace had the letter "K" dangling. She introduced herself as Katerina.

"So, you boys heer for good time," she asked, her hands now, warmly, on each of our thighs. It's only in strip clubs that the women are more forward than men.

"Oh yeah. Always, eh," said Eric, as he took another sip of beer.

She chewed her gum with big yawns. She feigned disinterest and looked around, pretending she wanted to find someone better.

"I like your tattoos," said Eric. She had them all over her legs.

"I want to giet another one," she said. "I have idea for Phoenix going up from ash with rose, you know rose, flower, all around."

"Actually, I'm only a Graphic Design student, but my friend here, he's the real deal…," Eric said, gesturing his thumb toward me.

"Den you kan do it for me," she asked.

Eric put his arm around me, dragging me forward into the conversation.

"So, buddy, what do you think?"

I looked in Katerina's eyes, her fake pink contact lenses, and I thought deeply about what she asked for, visualizing it in my mind. It was symbolic, the rising of a Phoenix, wings spread wide on fire. Beneath the turbulent bird lay everything she left behind. Transcending past her body into thin smoky air. The roses representing love and all its many faces.

And then it hit me, "Wouldn't the roses burn up?"

Eric slapped his forehead. There was no helping me.

This kitty purrs all night. She's a pussycat with a tail that won't quit. Just looking for a post to scratch. Fellas, give it up for… Katerina!

The DJ's announcement drowned out my last comment.

"That is me, boys! I must go!" Katerina shot up from the cushion. I watched her ass and glass heels shimmy to the stage.

Eric stared at me and said, "What's the matter with you, man? I tried to get you a commission, or at least a lay."

"Why are we even here," I asked him. "I thought you already have a girlfriend."

We were in the woods. It was cold and it was grey. The light was still out. The sun, buried in the clouds, glowed ever slightly violet.

Dad stood there in his overalls. The single barrel shotgun swinging gently by his side. He loaded two red cartridges into the chamber and pumped the action.

We were up the road from the house, past the next house over. It was likely someone's property but it was wooded. We parked the metallic blue Ford Ranger on the side of the gravelly road and lost ourselves among the birch trees. My lungs took in the smell of dry wood. The air was misty but different than the foggy countryside of Eastern Europe. Once we settled in a little clearing, I looked around for witnesses. Nothing but bark on trees and leaves blowing in the wind. And silence. Dead, quiet, silence.

"*Trebuie să înveţi...*" he said. You need to learn.

"I need to learn what," I asked. "Am I required to hunt my own groceries from now on?"

American westerns on TV made him think that this was lawless country, out here in rural Ontario. There was a thrill to it all. He was acting as a mentoring father, thinking this is what he had to do. We both were first generation. But he came late in life. That made the difference.

"You can take the first shot and all dat," he said. "Remember, never keep it pointed to anyone and never point it to yourself."

He handed it to me.

"Just shoot it into any tree. But not too close. Remember there's gonna be a big kick and all dat."

Only thirty minutes earlier, it was laying on his sofa, rolled up in a stained canvas like a French crepe. Laid out was a 12 gauge shotgun. The pump action was an orange wood with varnish. Same with the stock. The barrel and the receiver were stainless black steel. The ejection port and trigger were polished silver.

"What on earth are you doing with that," I asked, when he unraveled the damned thing.

"A man needs protection," he said, like out of a movie.

From what exactly, the old man had no answer.

Now, surrounded by woods, he wanted to show me how to use it. I raised it carefully to my eye level.

"Hold it firmly against your shoulder," he said. "Brace yourself for the kickback and all dat."

The crackling of the leaves beneath our feet had silenced. The trees no longer whispered. Father and I stopped talking all together. If there were animals among those dry and wrinkled trees, they were mighty quiet. They hid behind the browns, the greens, the muddy greys.

I kept trying to find a comfortable position of the stock against my right shoulder. With my left eye closed, I searched through the sight for something. Anything. There were no birds, no squirrels, no creatures. Just trees. I picked one at random. The poor innocent. My barrel settled at eye level on the tree and my finger tightened against the trigger. Every muscle in my back and shoulders tensed.

Something busted, splintered, far away, and my shoulder almost broke off. The impact threw me backward, with the barrel of the shotgun shaking wildly. Powdery smoke floated in the air. What was once fresh leafy air now smelled like charred steak and sulfur. It was hard to hear beyond the lingering bass, ringing from the firearm.

That it would be this loud was unexpected. The sound embarrassed me, like when my dad dragged me into Giant Tiger to buy jeans when I was thirteen. I wanted to blend into the nature of Canada. He wanted to make his individual mark. Although I never thought anybody would come in after us (we were wielding a shotgun, after all), our neighbours knew. They knew whoever fired were crazy. Who in their right mind would shoot a firearm in an area that was clearly not for hunting? We were in a season out of season.

Paralysis overtook me. I wanted to forgo the whole thing before we even got out here. But I couldn't. I had to feel like a man. This is what men do. They shoot guns, amid the dry and weathered trees.

The old man could tell I was shocked by the experience. We looked at each other and breathed out laughter.

"You... you wanna shoot," I asked, giving away all my feelings about the experience.

"I don't have to," he said, laughing.

"Thanks."

We drove back to the house. The whole while he was teasing me at being shaken up. The ringing lingered in my ears. I grinned like an idiot and took the quips. There was no thrill to be had. Not for me. Wondering why hunters hunted, I reasoned, it wasn't that they loved to hunt as much as they loved to be afraid. It was all about overcoming one's fear. Beating out the intervals of your pumping heart.

Back at the house, I sat beside the old man eating leftover cabbage rolls with sour cream, both of us watching TV.

"T-sa fost frica, uh?" So you were scared, eh?

He kept laughing.

I came down the stairs. The morning breeze followed the light into the living room through the open porch door. The mist of the dark was gone and my vision was sharp in the bright natural air.

Dad was where I left him last night. He always slept on the couch with the TV on.

"Take a look at this. I brought you something." I pulled it from my messenger bag and handed it to him. It was a letter-sized magazine. It was perfect bound. Black and white. Even the cover was black and white. The words were in Romanian except for a few English words.

"Look, it says 'Story Book Business.' I think it was for some college course back in Romania. It's dated 1986. During Ceaucescu's time."

Dad leafed through it with his thumb. He could see the articles were sparse, with some pages spaced like a poetry anthology. The whole newsprint pamphlet was merely seventy pages.

"Where did you find this?" He asked. His voice raspy with the smoke blowing out.

"Eric found it at the Stittsville Flea Market. He gave it to me. I think it was for some business course back in Romania."

His expression changed from curiosity to wit.

"The thing about Romanians," he said with a dismissive airy wave and smirk, "as soon as they have a first grade education and all dat, they on the search for somebody dumber. *Dumb and dumber*. They so badly want to show everyone how smart they are. As soon as a Romanian graduates from kindergarten, he immediately wants to teach the same class."

He handed it back to me. I said, "You keep it. I brought it for you."

He said, "I learn enough."

"You think I'll learn about business from this," I asked him jokingly.

"If you have to depend on Romanians to teach you business and all dat, I pray for you. We all are in trouble."

"Everything is a struggle" he said. "It's down from inside," he pointed to his sternum. Meaning: If you don't have turmoil in your life, you must create it. That's the only way to motivate yourself to keep on going. That was his definition of life.

Cold War, an abusive father, and a mentality that everyone was against him.

When he moved out here to Canada, he pushed away everyone, like *leave me alone*, in the belief that no-one could love him. His perspective on life didn't make it so desirable to start a family, which was his new initiative.

I argued with him. "If everything is a struggle, what's the point of anything?"

"I want you to settle down and all dat, so I can see you being a man. Not because I want you to struggle. The everyday bullshit is part of everything and all dat, but this *miserable* life is still worth it." He had this way of saying mi-se-ra-ble, pronouncing every syllable.

My argument wasn't that I didn't want to do it. It was that "I insist on doing it in my own time." To him, time was universal. It only went forward and eventually the coils would unravel gravely. I just didn't want to hear about the pressure of time.

"There's a right time to do something." That was as much as he thought about the time we have on this Earth. His perspective was finite. "I don't want you to miss the boat." Then he made it into a joke, "The boat is leaving. Hello," he waved at me.

"Everyone is doing things later now," I told him. Another question still remained, "Why even mess around with women, if you claim you have not met a good one and my mom was the worst?"

"I didn't say she was the worst. You have to form your own opinion and all dat. For dat matter, your grandmother was a saint. Dat was one good woman."

"It all sounds contradictory to me," I said with a coy look on my face, like I was making trouble. Intentionally putting a person on the defensive was my tactic for winning a debate. To get the other person to exhaust their argument. Hoping by the time they were finished, I'd have a good rebuttal.

"Life isn't a debate, Alex. Life is bitter and cold and sexy and sometimes you have to slap it in the face and beat your chest like a gorilla." He made a karate chop slap gesture and banged his fists on his chest.

"Dostoyevsky couldn't've put it better himself," I teased him.

"You laugh but I read all dat. I read thousands of books. That's all I did before I met your mother. I educate myself."

"I know. You recommended Dostoyevsky to me. I read *Brothers Karamazov* in college. Read it again last year." I didn't tell him how beyond it was for me the first time. Now I had some opinions. "I don't consider Dostoyevsky an author," I declared. "He channeled his characters. The way they spoke was like it was transcribed. The words on the page. But I guess that's the style of the Russian writers."

With that statement, I took the fun out of the conversation.

"It is rude to challenge the host of the house," he said with a royal air. It was a dismissive joke but also a life lesson, for when I'm out in public. Don't be a smart ass. It's smarter to be smart and not have to show it.

I went to the garage to paint for a couple of hours.

"I want you to find a nice girl from a good family," he said, "with a good dowry and all dat."

His thick yellow fingers pinched a cigarette. In the other hand he had a coffee. He took a drag, inhaled, then coughed. His stormy eyes were hidden behind cheap bi-focal glasses with the line across. He had white hairs among his mostly blonde mane. His bushy moustache hovered over his upper lip, hiding his brown teeth. The back ones were gold. When I was younger, his hair had been shorter, almost as short as mine, but as time passed, he let it grow enough to hide most of the lines on his forehead. My concept of him was as a brave strong man. Sometimes in my mind he was like a wise prophet. In the sentimental moments, he was a sweet and loving dad. Like a wolf with his cub. And other times he just served as my father. A pure formality.

He had flaws and I still worked on forgiving him.

"I been lookin'," I told him.

He touched my face, like that's my boy. His hands were hard, from years of labour.

At home, he mostly spoke Romanian to me. I answered in English. I thought in English. Romanian was my reptilian brain, hardwired, with English built on top. Dad was a Romanian through and through. His mind was speaking English with the dictionary open. Maybe, over the years, this was the reason for the breakdown in communication.

"Not like your mother. She had nothing. Her family was no good. On top of dat, she was a whore."

The conversation about my mom always came up at least once every visit and I tried to avoid it.

"But tell me how you really feel."

"I fought for you. I was the only one who wanted you. I wanted many children, but she only gave me one. And then she cheated on me every chance she got. I don't even know for sure if you're mine."

She did this. He did that. There was a time when hearing him talk this way about my mother angered me. Now, my emotions were kept at a distance. This made him say outrageous things to bring up my feelings. When someone's insecure about your love for them, their last resort is to twist your face toward a common enemy.

"That is why I turned to drinking and all dat. She drove me to it," he continued.

"But you're clean now," I told him, trying to focus on the positive.

"Yes, I am clean. I am on the bandwagon and all dat."

"The wagon. You're on the wagon," I corrected him. He didn't get it.

"I am sober for four months." His hands were shaking.

"And let's keep it that way. You work yourself up every time you mention her."

"Don't defend her."

"I'm not defending her."

"It was the same with Jessica."

I moved away from him, busying myself with some near-by wood planks.

"Let's just do these stretchers."

The studio was in an insulated garage separate from the house. It fit one big car, with space around and had a private toilet. We also installed a wood oven in the corner, to heat the place in the Winter. I paid dad $500 a month for the studio. I wrote it off as a business expense. He resented the gesture. It implied our relationship was transactional. However, he needed the money. It helped with his mortgage.

"She was always on my case."

"You're still talking about mom?" I plugged in the table saw.

"No. Jessica. She tried to control me and all dat."

"She was my girlfriend, dad."

Jessica was a closed chapter in my life but parents give birth and they also unearth.

"Why is it her business to tell me how to live my life and all dat?"

He didn't let it go because he knew I blamed him for the breakup.

"I know you blame me and all dat but you pushed her away. Not me. Jessica did not love you. She was in love with the idea. She never love you for who you are."

He propped the stretchers on the table with his left hand, a cigarette in his fingers. His other hand sanded off the slivers.

"And who am I exactly?"

"I understand why you pushed her away and all dat. You wanted her to love you for you. But you made one mistake my son."

I picked up a strip of sand paper and joined him in the sanding.

He continued.

"You pushed her too far away and all dat. She never found her way back. You must live with dat and move on. Find a new woman and all dat."

I thought of a short story I read called *Peasants* by Chekhov. A middle class man with his wife and kids had to move back with his family who were peasants. All of them complained constantly and the elders nagged and belittled the young ones. Their words were vulgar and cruel to each other and their insults piercing. But they kept busy all the time, cooking, farming, begging, and so on. They walked on dirt floors in their unfinished home. When I thought of the way that my dad spoke, I thought of that story. He grew up poor in a small village. I wondered if richer families were kinder to each other.

When my dad switched on the band saw, I jumped. He spared no look to my reaction. Instead he focused on his job cutting the pine into neat slabs. I steadied the ends of the pieces. Ash fell from the cigarette poking out from under his yellow mustache. His hands were steady now.

The knock and the voice hit at the same time.

"Hey, John." That was my dad's name in English.

It was Nick calling, with his daughter Sophie hand in hand, in the doorway of the open garage. Nick was a muscular man and had long blonde hair. Sophie had really chubby cheeks and her eyes were sparkling auburn. She had her platinum blonde hair done up in ponytails, with cartoons on her hairbands. She'd been in my studio before. She looked around in wonder, taking in an inventory of anything new.

"Hello Neighbour."

My father turned into a different person. The smile that spread across his face was contagious and the room felt brighter than it did when we were alone.

"How's the new job?"

"Is going good. I been there two months."

"Jarvis is a good company. And you're union now."

"No. Not yet," said dad. "I must wait ninety days. If I do not miss a day for ninety days, then I get my union card and all dat."

Nick said, "That'll take no time. No problem."

"Hello sweetheart," dad said to Sophie. She scrunched her neck and giggled. "Are you married yet?"

"Nope," she replied, "I'm not old enough to be married."

"How old are you, anyway?"

"Six and a half," she blushed. She showed him her open palm plus one thumb.

They went on like that, until she asked, "Is that your painting?"

"Is it okay?" her father asked me, his hands on Sophie's shoulders.

I said, "Absolutely." She ran to the far end of the studio, where I had several paintings leaning against the wall. One of them was an attempt to bring to life the woods beyond the house. She was fascinated by the picture, and kept pointing and touching. It was unfinished but dried since the last time I painted. Sophie was gesticulating but I had no clue what she was saying. Something about finger painting at school. All children are artists, I thought. Only some give up their dreams as adults. To keep the dream alive, I offered to let her finger-paint on a small piece of paper I had lying around. She was thrilled. That kept her focused. I encouraged her, as I did with my students in class.

"By the way, I'll bring back the table saw as soon as we're done," my father said.

"No rush. Use it as long as you like. It's not why I came over…" I shot him a thankful nod, realizing that the saw was for my *little* art projects. "I just came to say I saw the sign you did for No Frills." Nick continued, looking over at me and Sophie.

"You mean in Prescott and all dat? Yes, I did the whole thing from tits to ass."

"I might need a little help with the shed I'm building. Just some advice really."

Dad jumped at the change to help Nick. He loved to be needed.

"Anyway, I was just seeing about the new job and all that," said Nick. The "all that" was contagious.

"The job is great," my dad replied. "The only bad thing is dis guy at work…"

Sophie said something and I turned my ear back to her, to supervise her finger painting. She was delightful and curious. Her tongue stuck out a little between her lips as she concentrated.

I couldn't help pick off some pink acrylic paint and dab her nose with it. She let out a huge laugh that lit the whole garage. Both dad and Nick were tickled. Dad because he wanted me to have one of my own and Nick because their child's joy is what a good parent lives for.

"It's easy to clean from your hands and face," I told her, "But don't get it on your clothes."

Nick's Mrs. called them in for lunch and Sophie skipped off with him to their house across the street. I heard her tell him it was super fun.

Dad and I finished cutting the stretchers. He was set to go in the house. He asked me in but I told him I was gonna hang back for a few minutes to study my art.

"Dad," I said, before he left. "Is something going on at work?"

"Everything is okay."

"Alright, 'cause I heard you saying something to Nick."

"There is a young guy on my ass and all dat. He thinks because I have accent I am stupid too. Other den dat, you know me, just fucking the dog."

He went in and I was left with the images.

Sophie left behind her picture. It's funny how kids leave artworks behind or they gift them. Very few kids are materialistic. There were portions of it that were so thick they were still wet. The page was covered with *all* the colours in an abstract pattern. Her signature took half the page.

The moment held me in a daydream, at the foot of the garage. It was much warmer now and I was sweating from trimming the stretchers. I could see clear across the open field to the edge of the forest where earlier we shot the gun. The soft breeze whispered, as I squinted, looking for life. A pair of cardinals rose above the trees and dove back down.

"Hey, comrade! *Ce mai faci?*"

A voice I knew too well called out for me. Parting the sea of people was Constantin, one of my closest friends from high school and a fellow Romanian. He was clad entirely in black, just like I remembered him. We were the same height but he had filled up in his shoulders and his stomach with hard muscle, like an Iron

Shiek. His long hair, dyed black, was tied into a ponytail.

"I been hearing some cool shit about you, comrade," he said.

"Just plugging away," I said, playing modest.

The event was at a packed three story building, in a wide-laned residential area. It was gutted on the first floor and refashioned into a gallery space with high ceilings. Little pieces everywhere adorned the walls. Price labels were inconsistent since each artist brought their own. There was a band playing music with a pretty singer wearing laced fingerless gloves. A river of colorful hairstyles, leather, and blue jeans flowed around me as I did live painting in the corner. That's how Constantin found me.

"I heard about your last exhibit. Sorry I missed it," he said.

"It's cool. It was only a group show," I told him. It's hard to admit to people that when they say they'll *try to make it*, I secretly wish that they do. "I'm trying to land a solo," I added.

"Comrade. Talk to JP."

What a genius.

"Really? Hadn't thought of that." Of course I thought of that. That's why I was here. Trying to bank up these group shows and get a solo.

Then a crash was heard, like on queue.

"Hey, you fucking guys! Come on! You're cleaning that," JP was yelling.

Constantin and I looked in the direction of the noise. My eyes fell on a brunette. She had her neck turned to the commotion. When she panned her eyes back through the crowd. She caught my stare. I thought quick and sent her a wink. Her cheeks popped with a smirk.

That's all I needed. Our glance was long enough for a connection. Short enough so it wasn't strange. I turned back to Constantin. His mouth was moving but there was no sound. A dumb grin crept on my lips. Her image stood etched on the inside of my blinking eyelids. To his credit, Constantin completely disregarded my distraction.

"I'm working for the government," I heard him say. "My mother hooked me up."

Should have known.

"Right. She works at Stats Canada," I reminded myself aloud.

His focus darted to friends he spotted across the room and started waving.

"Comrade. Good to see you... I have to say hi to someone. But stick around. I have something we can share later," he said, showing me a glimpse of a little baggy of white powder. Then he snuck it back in his pocket. And he was engulfed by the crowd.

An impulse struck me to turn around and look for the girl. She was gone. I wandered through people with beers in their hands and found myself at the stairs and then up on the second floor. Smaller rooms were arranged upstairs as little galleries. Each room featured a single artist. The first room had portraits. The second was filled with JP's smaller works. If JP offered me one of these little rooms, I would never accept. My goal was to show big pieces in the main gallery downstairs.

Loud shouts came from JP's office. I pushed my way through the blockade of people in the narrow hallway.

"I paid you the full fucking thousand," JP shouted, gesturing with his hands.

"I only got half. You still owe me five hundred," the artist yelled back. He was a thin guy with arm tattoos and piercings in his ears.

"Fuck you. I remember I gave you cash," JP said, louder than before.

The onlookers turned away, busying themselves. They didn't want to get involved.

"You definitely didn't. Trust me. I would know if I had money," the artist said, turning his torso to one side, as though bracing himself for a fight.

"This isn't the night, man. I'm having a fucking party," JP said.

"Well, I need to get *fucking* paid," the artist said. He wasn't budging.

"I fucking paid you, man."

To ingratiate myself to JP, I decided to intervene, before things got physical. But in truth I didn't know whose side to take. I went through this with the community center, trying to get paid. I sympathized with the artist but I also needed to stay on good terms with JP.

This altercation spoke to the way JP did business. He didn't keep any record of transactions. Now they had an argument of what each one remembered. Of course the artist remembered being owed money and JP having settled everything, each in their own best interests.

"Don't you guys have any proof or receipts," I asked.

"No. We did it off the books," the artist said. "It was his idea."

"Man, I was doing you a fucking favor. After all I sold for you."

"This is bullshit," said the artist.

"You know what? Let me put this politely," said JP. I thought, for a second, things might work out. He said, "Go fuck yourself. You're not showing here no more."

Arguing was one thing, but to do it so publicly about money was embarrassing for the witnesses too.

I stepped in between JP and the young artist. Other attendees huddled around.

"Don't trust this guy," said the artist, shooting me a glare.

"Throw his fucking ass out of here," said JP.

The artist kept yelling, "Bullshit, fucking bullshit." He walked away down the hall. Everyone slowly dispersed.

"That's pretty crazy," I said.

JP said nothing. Just sat behind his desk. I took a chair opposite him, scared to say the wrong thing and set him off again. JP was shifting piles of paper off his desk into a drawer.

"We're living in a work society," he finally spoke. "It's an all out, all or nothing, life. But these fucking artists, they wouldn't understand that."

Pointing out that he's also an artist might have been the wrong thing to highlight so I kept my mouth shut. I just watched his actions nervously.

JP was a tall mouth-breathing Viking with freckles and bad teeth. He taught himself art and made a killing in New York when the art market was hot. He came back to his hometown Ottawa and bought this house two years ago. Turned it into a gallery. He had all sorts of complaints from his neighbours due to the noise. The city questioned the legality of a commercial space in a residential area. He argued that he worked from home and the receptions were private parties, with alcohol of course. So far, he was still in business.

He recomposed himself with a breath. "What can I do for you, Alex?"

"Just wanted to say congratulations,"I told him. "Great reception," I added, buttering him up. "I love the scale of your pieces." Maybe I was overdoing it, I thought.

"Thanks man. Good to be appreciated. Unlike these ungrateful leeches," he said projecting his voice out in the hallway.

I took a deep gulp of air and went for it.

"Yeah, I've been working on a new series," I told him. "I'd love to show you sometime."

"Definitely. Send me some JPEGs," he said.

"It's similar to the piece I'm painting tonight, but some are very large scale. Bigger than yours," I said. This last line irritated the competitor in him. PJ taught himself art late in his twenties. Despite his technical shortcomings, he still sold more than anyone who showed in his gallery. "I'm just about ready for a full show," I announced. I gauged his reaction carefully. He didn't say anything for a few seconds, before looking back beyond me to the open door.

"I've got another group show coming up. We'll try a small piece," he told me.

"I'm interested in a solo," I clarified.

"Listen, Alex," he said, beginning to get irritated. "You're a great guy, but your work doesn't sell. I only sold one piece by you in the last year. And that was the very first one I hung."

He was right. Most of the sales were of his own work. That was the trouble with artist-owned galleries. They sold their own work first. "I sell pieces," I said. "Not all of them at your gallery. But I sell pieces. My work is original. I think that's the problem. I'm trying to *innovate*."

My voice cracked with the last line. He looked at me like I was lying to myself.

"Innovators struggle. *Workers* sell," he said. "If you want success as an artist, Alex, you must learn to sell."

When you're drowning in molasses, you think of all sorts of ways to justify your stupidity. You figure the world wasn't aligned in your favour. It was never my own fault, I thought.

"I have pieces in the MoMA, Alex," he continued. "I have pieces in the Whitney, L.A., London, the Tate. I know how to sell. I know how to networked. How do you think I got my own gallery? I've been in Christie's, Sotheby's, sold for over a million. I've played with the big boys. No offense, Alex, but you don't have it. You may never have it... *unless you learn to sell*."

"I am still figuring out my angle," I told him.

"It's more than that, man." He was like an impatient teacher now, with me as his anger's target. "You gotta network with people that can influence your career," he said. "If you're not in the room with those people, if you're not rubbing elbows with them, how the fuck could you be successful? Dumbass."

JP's own work was thick and crude, with bright oil pigments. His price tags reflected the high cost of his supplies. And he didn't let patrons forget how much he spent. He knew his worth.

I hated him.

"I'm going through a journey," I said, turning inward.

"I see," said JP. "So you're in your *Cubist blue period* phase. Looks to me like you're in your *loser* phase. Why don't you shut the fuck up with your self-indulgent piece of shit phase and prove to me you can sell."

"It's a *Catch-22*," I backfired. "How can I prove it? I need the opportunity. It's like, how do I get a job without the experience and how do I get the experience without the job?"

He laughed.

"While you figure out your shit, I gotta get back to the party," he said. "Bring a piece, maybe two. I'll try to fit you in the next group show. That's the offer. Now fuck off."

It was then I realized that raising himself as the cream of the crop involved stepping on other artists. Maybe it was that he didn't care or maybe it was just business. What he made me feel like was an imposter.

He shut his laptop and heaved himself off his desk. He grabbed his bottle of beer from the shelf next to the door. I watched him as he went on mingling down the stairs. He was back to his cheery self, grinning, laughing, making jokes with the attendees. His fight about money with the other artist was forgotten. My solo show proposal too was forgotten.

I felt queasy. My chest could not expand. I fought to breathe, like I was underwater, but I followed JP's lead out the door. Whether I could follow his professional lead or his attitude was another question entirely.

"There you are. Is there a bathroom around here, for us Comrades to have a private meeting?"

There was a spacious bathroom around the corner. "I think guests are supposed to use the one downstairs," I said.

"The one downstairs is filthy. We'll take this one. We can celebrate, like old times," he said, with a baggy of cocaine pinched between his fingers.

We ducked inside the bathroom. Nobody watching.

Constantin slicked his hair back and checked his teeth in the mirror first. He always had a feline personality. Slow movements. Always grooming.

"So you workin' for the government now, eh?" I asked, staring around at the fifteen squared foot bathroom. PJ's artwork hung above the toilet.

"Yeah. The job is new," he said, excited. "We're helping out Haiti who was hit by another hurricane. I'm in the task force assigned to that. It's really great to make a difference."

"I heard there was a lot of corruption."

"No. They're doin' alright," he said, a little startled by my negativity.

"I'm happy you're excited," I recovered.

"They got me on probation right now, 'cause I just started. But once I'm in, all I gotta do is put in twenty-five years and I can retire with a good pension."

"Twenty-five years, eh?" Twenty-five years to life, I thought. Sentenced.

"Maybe thirty, depending on how much money I want when I retire." These weren't his original ideas. It was a path set out by many others before him. Devote your life to public service and retire with a good pension. Enjoy your life in the moonlight hours of the day and save your dreams for the sunset years of your life. He was already thinking like his mom. She too sacrificed an engineering career, to work for Stats Canada.

"Okay, so you'll be about sixty. What are you gonna do then?"

"Whatever I want."

"Don't you think it's a shame?" I asked.

"How?"

"You have the talent to do whatever you want… now," I flattered him.

"Thanks man but I like the benefits. I'm pulling in six figures and own a condo with a view of the Ottawa River." He laughed as he produced a small rectangular mirror from his pocket.

Everything made sense now. Life is a helluva burden for most men. We need to drink to numb the emptiness of existence and drugs to quicken our heartbeats to live in the moment. Without a stable career, there's no legitimate way to buy the stimulants to make life worth living. He figured it out. He traded the pursuit of his art for a career that fed his immediate needs.

I sat on the toilet with the lid down, watching him tap his finger on the open edge of the little ziplock bag. From the transparent plastic, white powder fell onto his little mirror. There was great anticipation on Constantin's face. His profile looked like a Grecian-period Picasso. The way he concentrated on the lines of cocaine impressed upon me the vision of a man trapped within a ceramic vase. One slip and he could shatter on the floor.

At Canterbury, we tried weed and even LSD and PCP. While I stopped with stimulants, to have my art unhindered by abstraction, he continued using. He read Timothy Leary and we both gawked over the art of Moebius and H.R. Giger - their art inspired by psychedelics. We jokingly admired punk rockers and goths, like Sid Viscous, Billy Idol, and Andrew Eldridge - their recklessness, their depth-diving, what we perceived their *joie de vivre*. I saw those interests as a way to scare our parents. He saw them as a guide to heighten living.

Constantin's blood was of the type like Byron and Shelly. He was a scribbled poem in draft form, bleeding on the parchment from a quill.

Our ambitions diverged. Constantin pursued distractions from ennui, while I developed my artistic skills in school. Once I started college, we met rarely except one time a couple of months before the incident. When I saw him that time, we drank cappuccinos on a Bank Street patio. We drew on napkins and exchanged ideas. He was dating a goth girl at the time. She popped by, at the end of our meeting. She wore thick-soled black Doc Martins and had a cute face, powdered white, with piercings in her nose and lip. They had a small apartment on Gladstone. She worked part-time at an erotic book store. He lived from an allowance from his parents.

The incident in question was a spell of paranoia. Some stranger at the club was flirting with his girlfriend and Constantin followed him outside. The clueless dude was having a smoke next to the neon entrance, when a shifty Constantin pulled out a switchblade and stabbed him in the gut.

The *stranger* lived. They went to court. Constantin's parents' lawyer helped reduce the sentence to probation, as a first offense.

As briefly as I laid it out, Constantin recited it over the phone one night when I was graduating college. He was in a dark place. In an attempt to tear through the tightening shroud of his existence, he had become dangerous. Everyone distanced themselves, including his girlfriend whom he never saw again.

He was dating a new girl now. I hadn't met her yet. He outgrew the downtown scene, since he got himself a respectable job. The external stimulants hadn't disappeared entirely. They just came in a more sophisticated form. No more five dollar hits of acid.

I understood his past and present. All of it was now unspoken. My reminiscence was replaced by Constantin's credit card tapping his mirror. A red fifty dollar bill lay on the sink beside him.

A black and white photo of a church above the towels reminded me of the good old days. "You still have that photo," I asked him. "You know, the one with the balloons on the sides."

"Yeah, yeah. My mother gave me that Polaroid."

"It was themed like a birthday party."

"We were bad-ass leaning against the cathedral doors with black leather jackets, studded belts. True irony."

"It always made me laugh," I said. "We ran a bit of a cult in high school, didn't we? We were the 'Trenchcoat Mafia' without a manifesto. It was a dark joke but some of my best memories."

"Oh, you remember Chris?"

"Of course," I laughed. "Chris was always a real hustler." Chris made a creative living like me. He worked gigs ghostwriting books and publishing his own material. "God, I haven't seen him in a while. Is he still writing?"

"He's dead," said Constantin.

"Are you serious?"

"Yeah."

Two lines of coke were up his nose already.

"Don't fuck with me."

"I was at his funeral last month. I thought of you but I didn't have your number. It was a small affair."

"God. What happened?"

"Suicide," he said, licking his gums and sucking his teeth.

I had to reflect for a moment.

"But he was doing so good," I said.

"He was for a while. It looked that way. He had the blog. He made the videos. Then he fell in love with some girl online and she broke his heart I guess. She blocked him on social media. Stopped taking his calls. It all spiraled within a week."

"Holy shit."

"He wrote a crazy blog before he ended it. A suicide letter."

"Did you read it?"

"Yeah. His mother took it down after the funeral. I'm glad I ran into you. I almost forgot about it."

He almost forgot about it. I let out a breath of laughter.

"How's it possible to forget about something so tragic," I asked.

"People move on," he said.

That hit me hard. If I died tomorrow, would I be forgotten next week? Here I was fighting for my artwork to be seen and represented. Fighting to be thought of and remembered. And people move on. They forget.

The fifty dollar bill was now held together tightly in my fingers.

"Your turn," he said.

In the sculpture garden, she was completely immersed in a work of art. I made very slow and very quiet steps to see exactly what. She stood in the middle of two abstract sculptures. The force of her silhouette held all space around her, like Samson between the pillars. She balanced everything. From the back, there was a wash of blue across her body. She was facing a pedestal. The piece upon it was a heart of iron, wired to an outlet next to the house. The mechanisms made the heart beat like a clock. It was steel grey and expanded and contracted like a real pulsating heart. It sounded like an old film reel, amping up my nerves as I approached her.

"The heart of a blue whale can fit two people in it comfortably," I said. It was the best line I could come up with.

She turned and paused, and asked, "Are you a scientist?"

"No. I'm just a nerd," I said.

She ducked her smiling face behind her shoulder-length brown hair. While turned to the side to see me, her brown eyes caught sight of the other men in back of me, hanging near the exit, watching her initially. Now watching us. Their eyes darted and their feet changed direction. They all fled inside. I was left alone, as Cupid's only spokesman.

"My name is Alex."

"Laura," she said, lending me her hand.

The smell of her brand name perfume told me she was too good for me from the start. She carried herself with a stiff poise that could make most men's knees buckle. Some wildebeests could stand up to a lion or kick a crocodile's bite. It was like she travelled the jungle with a horde behind her. Yet she stood alone.

"You ever dated an artist," I asked.

"No. Can't say I have," she said.

"You like art?"

"Sure. Who doesn't?"

"You'd be surprised," I said.

I followed up by getting her to talk about herself. She told me she's visiting. Had only been here a week. She's been living in Léon, France, and came to Ottawa for a French language course. She would only be here for a few months. Perfect. I hadn't thought that far ahead.

"What are you doing Thursday?"

"Probably studying," she said.

"Let's grab a beaver tail down in the Byward Market."

She held her answer back, analyzing me.

"It's not a real beaver. Don't worry," I joked.
"Comes with cinnamon sprinkles." She knew. "I know a good coffee place too. Puts Paris to shame," I said, totally bluffing.

She giggled. We smiled into each other's eyes.
She said, "Okay."

. . .

"Ready for your tour, *mademoiselle*?"

She greeted me on Parliament Hill. She was in a red flower dress.

"I got it in Paris," she said. "It's a Jean Paul Gaultier. He's my favorite designer. I paid 1,200 Euros for it. It took a long time but worth every penny."

I kissed her cheeks. "It's a French-Canadian custom," I told her. She smelt of complex and elegant florals.

Laura stood next to the Centennial Flame, feeling the monument's warmth. She brought up a quarter from her designer purse.

"We don't take American quarters," I said. She laughed and flicked it into the shallow water. I didn't ask. Her wish, lost among the pennies, nickels, dimes, and quarters. Looneys and Tooneys too. The flame beat on above the rich water.

We walked together.

We passed the war memorial on Elgin Street and I led her into the lobby of the Chateau Laurier hotel.

"Half the city had their graduation here," I told her.

She asked about my prom date. "Was she the one that got away, Alex?"

"Maybe," I told her. "She's probably settled down by now and living in a shoe," I joked.

73

"Down boy!" A voice came, just then. A fluffy brown poodle jumped up on Laura's dress. He was muddy. Laura began rubbing the stains out. She excused herself to the washroom to clean her dress and freshen up. The lady was apologetic, saying, "I'm still training him."

"It's hard enough without cute puppies vying for her attention," I said, patting the dog's head and feeling embarrassed for Laura making a big deal. When I was interested in someone, I always ignored the red flags. Her high end fashion sense and careful self image made me wonder what she was all about.

The Greeks thought love was a form of madness. Feelings lie. We all let whatever we want to believe override what we see. To Ovid, love was warfare. You have to endure rain, cold, and long roads ahead. But Ovid also recognized the pleasure and the benefits of love.

The lady with the dog was gone when Laura came back out a little sour but looking fine.

"So your family's in France," I asked her.

"I've been living in Léon but I was born in New York," she said.

"Oh, you're American. I'm sorry, but this isn't gonna work," I said, pushing her away.

"I should have my certificate in three months," she said. "With that, I can teach French in Léon and stay as long as I like."

"Thank god you're going back. I don't want you to catch feelings," I said, teasing her.

"That would be a first," she laughed.

I asked Laura about her family. She hesitated for a moment. "We don't get along," she said.

"I see."

"My father and brother run a business in Connecticut," she said. "A paint company."

"Cool. What kind of paint?"

"They're called PaintX."

"Little round tubes. Black label?"

"That's right."

"I've used their products," I told her.

"I figured," she said. Then turned the subject to me. "What about you?"

"It's just my dad and me," I told her.

"You must be pretty close then."

"Pretty close, yeah."

"Where's your mother?"

"My mother... She's gone," I told her.

"I'm sorry,"she said. Laura understood my mother had died. I didn't correct her.

By the time we walked through the legs of Louise Bourgeois' spider, in front of the National Gallery of Canada, Laura and I were familiar. I told her about my father. "He works for a signage shoppe." And she told me about her hobbies. "Golf and horses."

We were worlds apart. Yet here we were, arm-in-arm, smiling and laughing together. Dating was fun, I thought.

Through the upward path and underneath the glass dome of the National Gallery, we started with the permanent collection.

"There are so few pieces here," she said. "At the *Louvre*, they're so cluttered with artifacts."

"Canada is still making history. We're still collecting," I said, secretly hoping my work would someday be in here.

"Trying to shake off colonialism, I suppose, and make *une nouvelle histoire*," she said. "It's sad,"she continued. "Pretty much all looted. Every museum has a terrible history of stealing artifacts from the greatest civilizations on earth. With a legacy as thieves, how can western culture be considered anything but brutal?"

"But we preserve this art, don't we? I've seen footage of revolutions overseas with people knocking statues and destroying their history. If it wasn't for us, I mean, all the great works of art would be destroyed," I said.

"Ha! You're confusing colonialists for conservationists," said Laura. "Whenever you see a statue without arms or legs, it's not because time wore the artwork down. Looters either chopped off the statue from the legs up or they cut off arms or heads to sell separately. It's up to each civilization to decide what they do with their own artifacts. Many of the Asian statues for example are religious icons. So we're effectively stealing icons that priests and communities look towards for prayer."

"I thought they purchased all these," I said, as we moved into a gallery of Indigenous art. "We've been trying hard in recent year to focus on our own history, by exhibiting Native artists. The National Gallery still displays the Group of Seven, but some galleries like the Gallery of Ontario has removed Tom Thompson works, in favour of more ethnic artists. What do you think about that," I asked her.

"Good," she said. "At least they're trying. Maybe those works will *bleed* out to private collectors through auction houses. That will pad the pockets of the colonial galleries, which are publicly funded. Essentially, the governments are the ones buying and selling other people's cultural goods. Canada has a reputation as a nice country, Alex. In reality, they just have the least offenses."

We came upon a pile of bricks on bare gallery floorboards. The treatise written next to it on the wall was about the war in the Middle East.

"You're cute when you're political," I said, deflating the subject.

She got all serious and crinkled her nose. I kicked her leg. She punched me back then walked to the next room alone. I kept an eye on her from behind, giving her space. We went from room to room like that for about five minutes.

"Finally, the *Voice of Fire*," I announced. "The Louvre has the *Mona Lisa* by Leonardo Da Vinci. We have the *Voice of Fire* by Barnett Newman."

Laura thought I was joking for a moment but no.

"This was their big acquisition when the gallery opened. They paid $1.8 million in 1989. For three red and blue stripes. Locals still talk about it. Everybody says *they* could paint that."

"What do you think? You're the artist. Could you paint that," she asked.

"I could," I lied, "but I don't need the money."

After sharing a poutine in the Byward Market, we ducked into Cafe Deckuf, just as it was starting to rain.

The place had a bar, several tables, a few cushy lounge chairs in the corner, and a 15-foot stage. They hosted bands and also had a poetry night every Thursday.

"They call it Spoken Word," I told Laura.

"What's the distinction," she asked.

"Spoken word is more like a performance," I told her. "It's like Jazz, but with words. And it also makes you think, like poetry."

My friend Lilian Studt was taking five-dollar cover at the door and stamping hands. Her jazz duo *Cedrick* was comprised of her and her partner William Echard. They were scheduled to close out the poetry show with music.

"We're gearing up this year to have more gigs," Lilian told me. "If anything comes up, please let us know."

"I sometimes booked music acts for my art openings," I explained to Laura as we walked in.

Laura called me a "true bohemian."

"That's what everybody thinks," I told her, "But this is all business. It's all expensed out. You're on the corporate account, baby."

She got a laugh out of that but there was some truth. I was going to write off the gallery tickets from earlier and the drinks we'd have tonight.

We settled into an intimate booth in the corner. Droplets of rain decorated the darkening window. Laura sat against the cushions, facing the stage. I shifted my wooden seat to see the stage, as the performances began.

The first poet up was a pale girl with purple hair and thick granny glasses. They had fringes on the corners. We listened to her, as we scanned the stage and the vibe in the room. The blue and red stage lights double-lit her face. Her poem was confusing at first. It sounded like she was reading book titles. She was. *The Great Gatsby, In Cold Blood, Harry Potter*, an *Archie Digest*, a textbook on Social Sciences, and the list went on and on. She revealed it was a list of books on her ex-girlfriend's bookshelf.

You can tell a lot about a person's bookshelf. The first books that the poet recited were the famous titles. Authors she recognized. The books at the end of the list were either more obscure or controversial. At times, the titles were metaphors for her relationship with her ex. Like *Sophie's Choice* came at a point when she digressed about their situation. There was an autobiography of Donald Trump hidden away in the corner, near the bottom. She said it was a book her parents gave her. Another book was about family trauma as it's passed on through heredity. In the end, it was the books that were hidden away which caused conflict in their relationship. The things we carry with us which don't represent us truly. Even the junk books in our personal libraries linger in our personalities.

Laura smirked and raised one eyebrow.

I leaned in and whispered, "I'm not showing you my library."

She couldn't help but tell me about her love of books. Then asked me, "Do you read, Alex?"

"Of course I read, Laura."

"What do you read?"

"I read comics. Mostly for the pictures," I told her.

"So you like picture books, Alex?" She said busting my balls.

I played along telling her, "I'm up to a third grade reading level now."

"Oh la la, you're a big boy."

"You better believe it."

We laughed.

"I read some non-fiction and crime fiction too," I added, before turning the inquisition on her. "What about you?"

"Biographies and a lot of literary fiction. Some romance," she admitted, giggling.

The candle on the table tanned her face yellow. We talked about our favorite books from the poet's list. *Archie Digest* really resonated with her.

"When I was a little girl, granddad brought home little paperbacks. I loved them so much. I've been a fan of *Betty and Veronica* ever since."

"I learned English from Archie comics," I told her.

"Really?! English? What language did you speak before?"

I got good at introducing myself over and over, on these first dates. It was only recently I thought I needed a "logline," like a film description. An elevator pitch, in case I met my next lover in an elevator.

"I was born in Romania, actually."

"So you're Romanian?"

"By birth, yes. Canada has been my home for twice as long. Besides the food I had at home growing up, I feel more Canadian than Romanian."

"Do you speak the language?"

"At the level of an eight year old. You know, Romanian is very close to French. It's a Romance language. One of the five Romance languages. French, Italian, Spanish, Portuguese, and Romanian."

"*D'accord*," she said, figuring I'd understand.

"*De acord* would be the equivalent in Romanian. Means *to agree*."

"Of course," she translated. "It means 'of course.'"

"French is required here in Ottawa, with the government and all that." I caught myself in my dad's speaking pattern. "We're supposed to be bilingual," I continued. "I just lost interest in high school and haven't practiced since."

"You ordered poutine fine," she teased me.

"Stick with me, lady, and you won't starve," I said. And I gently flicked her chin upward, like we were starring in *Casablanca*.

We heard the next poet being called up on stage. He wore beads around his neck and wrists. Dressed in all black. Had a little peach fuzz goatee. He started speaking at a rhythmic pace.

"I ain't no provider," he said. "I got a lot on my mind-ah…"

I don't believe in matrimoney
I'm all about the mattress honey

Laura and I looked at each other. The delivery was stern and serious. But the tension released laughs among the audience. He went on for about three minutes.

It's in my nature, I'm a runner
Once you accept it, it'll be funner
I don't even know why you want me
Din't your parents warn you about me?

Laura laughed through the cringe.
Our love is now, not for evah
Sorry, I can't offer you bevah
If I could, I'd buy you dat ring
I'm upfront about what I bring

I ain't no provider, he said.

When he finished, he held out the mic and dropped it to the floor. He walked off stage into a crew of five guys at a front-row table. They cheered wildly, high-fives, and patted him on the back. One guy waved down the waitress to order his friend the poet a drink.

The cafe crowd loved it for being outrageous. Laura tried faking a laugh to fit in. I laughed it off, trying not to focus on the element of truth behind the comedy.

"Are you a provider, Alex?" She caught me off guard.

"Me? I'm an artist," I told her.

"Yes, I know you're an artist, Alex, but can you see yourself as a provider?"

This was a sore point but I took it on. "Being an artist is not an easy life," I told her. "It's not easy keeping a relationship."

"It's not?"

"Historically speaking. The artists I like, from the Renaissance, they were medians for god. Michelangelo, Da Vinci, both died as virgins. Rafael indulged himself and died of fever after love-making. He paid the price. Even Andy Warhol was a virgin till his sixties."

"I know you're not a virgin, Alex. What I'm asking is if you can provide for a woman."

"Great men don't know their abilities until they're tested," I told her. And then I added, "If love is on the line, I suppose I could be capable of anything."

"You're using language out of books, Alex. Let's be realistic."

84

"Oh, so you're traditional," I said, trying my best to deflect. "I understand. You need the support of a man."

"Quite the contrary," she said, offended. "I'm an independent woman."

"I get it, sweetheart," I said winking. "Things are hard nowadays."

"What if there were children?"

Laura was bringing out the heavy guns with heavy topics. I wasn't sure where her mind was going.

"My dear Laura, we just met," I said, making a joke of it again. Humour was my sole defense. "I want to keep things light," I told her. "But I'll be honest with you, Laura. I haven't given it much thought. I mean, it all depends on the couple I guess. You'd have to be able to negotiate who does what. I have friends where the roles are reversed. The female has a corporate job with benefits and he's the caregiver." I looked into her eyes and thought, I better tell her something good. "It all depends how the heart communicates between two souls," I finally said. "We have to get there, Laura. I *want* to get there *with you*, Laura."

I reached across the table and I touched her hand. She let me hold it, next to the candle warming our fingers.

She changed the subject, commenting how she liked the place I've chosen. When Laura dazzled me with her teeth, I mirrored her liveliness and cracked a few jokes, to bury her serious questions into the past. Her mood had flipped to a new page. Her eyes shimmered in the candlelight. Faint stage lights shifted colours on her cheeks.

The jazz duet came on. We listened to *Cedrick* for the first song and then we switched to chatting face-to-face. The sounds of electric piano and acoustic guitar became the soundtrack to our conversation. When the tempo was fast, our excitement matched it. When the music was smooth, we were romantic. Laura's words blended into the sounds. They danced through my ears. If it got too loud and hard to understand, I smiled and nodded and made sure she was comfortable.

I whispered in her ear, "Do you want another drink?" Her hair smelled like vanilla.

At the end of the night, as we were getting up to leave, I told Laura, "I changed my mind…"

"Changed your mind about what?" She was confused.

I held her breath with my words and said, "I thought about it and… I'd like to show you my library."

How hard a man waxes his bathtub before a woman's arrival is a clear indicator of his interest. The tub was scrubbed thoroughly, on hands and knees. I cleaned the floors around the toilet and all along the floorboards. The sink as well. My floss debris was polished off the mirror. "When it comes to love, clean for success," is what the lonely old slobs say.

I cleaned from the moment I got up. Good thing I did. Emily forgot her earrings on my bathroom counter. I tucked them away in my dresser drawer, underneath my folded socks, next to the condoms.

At one point, there was a ring on the intercom. Startled, I thought she arrived early and I wasn't ready. But it was a false alarm. Just a delivery man downstairs buzzing the wrong apartment number.

Soon-enough, I was changed, clean-shaven, and patting myself all over, wondering if I've missed anything.

Scented candles were lit.

I met Laura downstairs, in front of the building. She made the effort to come to my place and I didn't want her feeling nervous figuring out the front door buzzer or approaching my apartment door. Leading her up in the elevator, I reddened her cheeks with compliments. She wore hip-hugging jeans and a silk blouse. I kept her distracted from the stains on the second floor carpet. My gentle hand on the small of her spine led her careful steps over my threshold. She walked among my artworks, looking intimately at them in low light.

"These are amazing, Alex. I wish my family were artists," she said, as I handed her a glass of red wine. We clanked our glasses, sipped, and I excused myself back in the kitchen, tending to our dinner.

"What are you talking about? You come from a painting family," I called back.

"Making paint and making a painting are two different things," she said a little sadly. "Free spirits aren't allowed in free enterprise. My father's an industrialist. So is my brother. Neither can draw a circle. They can only draw blood."

The subject struck a vein, it seemed. I turned to the food.

The charcuterie was laid out on my work table which was draped with a checkered tablecloth. The presentation glowed in the corner under an ornate table lamp which I got at a garage sale for five dollars. A dating expert online said that when you're on a budget, there are little things you can do to make dinner at home seem fancier than it is. One of them was to serve caviar. In most large supermarkets, you can find a little jar of black caviar. Some *no name* cream cheese accompanied it, atop gluten-free sesame seed crackers. Sliced cucumbers, cherry tomatoes, and baby carrots balanced on one side, with a broken vine of grapes. Laura asked me to relax. She said I looked nervous explaining what everything was. She insisted I sit for a moment.

We talked about art.

"Where do you get your inspiration from?"

"My brain,"I told her, teasing. "Everywhere, really. Tonight is inspiring me quite a lot. How about you, Laura? What inspires you?"

"Lots of things. Flowers, animals, fashion. Lately it's a mix of Baudelaire and French New Wave cinema."

"Cool. Can't say that I've seen his films."

"Baudelaire's a poet, Alex."

My kitchen and living area were sparse. The desk and computer were in the corner, next to a tarped-off painting area. When I ate, I simply rolled my office chair to the table. Now, I gave Laura my chair, while I pulled up a stool.

The main course was fried salmon and risotto. All the while, we were smiling. She told me about her day of classes and about her roommate Joey. Apparently, he was a culinary student. She offered dinner at their place next time.

"So tell me why you're single, Laura."

"It's a mystery," she said. "Just haven't been focused on it, I guess."

"You must get asked out a lot."

"Once in a blue moon."

"How long you been single," I asked her.

"Oh gee. Must be well over a year," she said. "How about you?"

I lied and told her, "It's been several months." I raised my glass."Let's focus on us, tonight," I said. And then we clinked our forks into the last few bites.

I started washing the dishes, while Laura freshened-up in the restroom. She laughed at my obsessive compulsiveness, when she came out and saw me. She insisted I continue, while she refilled her glass with red wine. She then leaned against the counter beside me, twirling the wine in her glass like she owned everything. Her shoulders looked relaxed. Her cheeks were flush.

"I think the wine is getting to you, *mademoiselle*." I pretended to take her glass away.

For dessert, I gave her French vanilla ice cream. I shaved some orange-flavoured chocolate on top. We ate it slowly and talked intimately on the loveseat next to my dining room table.

"On working days," I told her, "This loveseat is a change of pace. Instead of drawing at the desk or at the easel, I slouch into the loveseat with my legs crossed. A pad and pencil on my knee. It reminded me of drawing as a kid. When I had finished my homework, I'd sit myself in front of the TV. My legs would be propped up on the coffee table, glancing up once in a while at the screen. I'd sketch like that till it was time for bed."

"Sounds like a lovely childhood, Alex."

"It was an escape," I said, revealing too much. "How would you describe your childhood?"

She took a while to answer, like her mind was sorting a box filled with assorted mementos.

"If I had to choose, my favourite memories were at my grandparents' cottage. Being on the lake. Sunbathing on the deck. Horseback riding."

Laura stared out, passionately, recalling her childhood. This left her exposed to admiration. When Laura turned her neck, a deep well was formed where her neck met her clavicle. There was nothing more I wanted than to drink out of that well.

She leaned into me, wanting to listen rather than talk. I stared into the reflections shimmering in her eyes.

A few minutes later, we were in my bedroom, fumbling with our clothes, almost toppling over my bookcase. She stubbed her toe on the foot of my bed. The pain turned to giggles at how clumsy we were. My kisses on her lips made it all better. Our pants came undone. Her blouse came off. She appeared vulnerable as she unbuttoned and slid off her bra. She looked down at herself, then back to me. The candlelight waves lapped on her breasts, looking like the hills of the Sahara desert. I knelt my dry famished lips to them. Her tight jeans were pulled down to the floor, the bottoms of her feet soon posted on my sateen sheets, as she reclined on my bed.

We were speechless but not without sounds. My fingers traced her back muscles, making them tighten with goosebumps. The side of her face pressed open-mouthed on my pillow. We rocked gently.

After some time, we lay there sweaty. Laura's head rested on my shoulder. She looked up at me, as with two fingers I parted her wet hair from her forehead.

I kissed her brow. She shut her eyes.

Her arm was on my chest. I strummed the back of her hand and forearm with my fingers. Normally, in moments like this, my heart would rush away like a bee fled a flower once pollinated. I'd leave before I was left.

It felt good to stay.

I mustered up the courage to say something romantic. From the heart. I needed to hear how it sounded, to know if it rang true.

"I like you Laura," I whispered with a lump in my throat. With no answer, I leaned in to see her face. She had fallen asleep.

Many minutes went by. My arm fell numb. My mind was awake with the words I said. They remained unrequited and it scared me.

With my free hand, I pulled the sheets over her lightly-beating chest, dislodging my sleeping arm in the process. As she rolled to her side under the covers, I slipped out to the restroom.

On the way back to the bedroom, I felt compelled to take up my leather bound sketchbook and my Palomino pencil.

The light of the moon pierced the blue drapes from one side of the bedroom and from the nightstand the flame from the candle flickered orange. The scent in the air was burnt lavender, mixed with us. Leaning back into the chair next to my corner bookshelf, I carefully observed Laura's face. Details that lay in the shadows came to the light of my eyes. My pencil was the translator. The brittle hand-made paper received the trailing curves through the graphite tip. With each line, time moved a little slower. In capturing the beauty of life, this little drawing threatened the night with endlessness. There wasn't a sound in the air, except for the scratching on the paper and Laura breathing.

My breath was nil.

When in the process of drawing, time slowed down. I could feel the earth dragging me along. To be aware of the seconds ticking was to realize that time could not be stopped altogether. And there was no going back. Life trajected only forward. My sole recoil was to slow down time to its present moment. In a relaxed state, an artist could snapshot the shift from past to present. That was what artists trapped on paper with a moment's sketch. A clip in time.

I drew Laura until my eyes became dry from staring. Her face pressed against the pillow was made more flattering by including her shoulders and a bit of the blanket too. This helped the drawing tell a story. A sleeping beauty.

When I got back into bed, Laura rolled toward me. I guessed this was instinctive. Before I fell asleep, the last thing I felt was the breeze from her breath on the pulse of my neck.

Light rustling was heard from the bedroom. Laura was getting up. I didn't rush her. She didn't rush to leave either.

She peeked her head into the kitchen and asked, "Mind if I take a shower?" Her hand was over her squinting eyes, blocking out the sun.

"Hey, good morning. Sure, it's all yours," I said.

"Smells good by the way."

The frying of the crepes spread the smell of vanilla through the entire apartment.

"Making some crepes for the mademoiselle."

"Oo la la. Can hardly wait."

As the shower ran, I thought my dad would like her. She was from a good family. I could already picture myself picking out colour swatches at her family's paint factory. Eric would like her too. She was attractive but not his type. So no real competition. It could be fun having Laura around. It felt good to have someone to make breakfast for.

I kept daydreaming like this, absorbed in the presentation of the breakfast. Two plates were set on my little dining table. Each of the flowery paper napkins had a knife and fork on top.

I heard the water stop.

"I'm out of the Canadian maple syrup," I said over my shoulder. "I can never keep it in the apartment long enough. But I have apricot jam. Rolled up with jam is how the Romanians eat it anyway. That or white sugar."

Some diced strawberries and cantaloupe were placed on the table in small bowls next to each of our plates.

"What kinda tea do you want?"

When she appeared, hair a little wet still, I fully expected compliments. Instead, she slammed the dining table with her palm.

Laura glared at me, as she lifted her hand from the table.

"There were more than one," she said. "I should be going."

She was all dressed and had turned toward the door. I looked back down at the table at the blonde hair as it lay wet and winding where her hand had been.

I jumped after her and pushed on the front door to keep it closed.

"It's not what you think," I said. Now that she was mad and leaving, I really wanted her to stay.

"I don't like being made a fool, Alex."

"It's a hair. It was nothing."

"Of course. It was nothing and I'm something. No thanks."

"I swear, Laura. She was just a girl that posed for my art. She got paint on herself. She had to take a shower. That was it," I tried to assure her, making it seem like almost nothing happened.

"Really?"

"Yes Laura. I swear." I grabbed her by the shoulders. Looked her in her eyes.

"I don't want you to think I'm the jealous type. I'm not. I understand you're an artist and you get a lot of opportunities. I just take exception to being lied to. There's no excuse for it," she said.

"Is this what you think I'm about?"

"I'm sorry," she said. "This isn't anything anyway."

"Don't say that," I told her. "It's too easy to just write it off. To end it before it begins. I mean you're only here for a couple of months anyway. But come on. Let's be adults here."

"I'm not used to jumping into bed like that."

"I like you, Laura," I told her again. I wondered now if maybe she had heard me last night and that scared her. "You got nothing to worry about," I said.

She fell, one shoulder against the door. Looked up at me. Her eyes darted back and forth between mine. She was searching for the answers to a dream.

"You know what," I said. "I'm actually getting upset now. It's not the damned hair. It's the damn crepes," I told her. "They're over there getting cold."

She disarmed, and smiled. Her shoulders, arms relaxed at her sides.

"Come on. Sit down. I made these for you," I said.

I kissed her on the left cheek, then the right.

"They do smell delicious," she said.

"Don't let them get cold," I told her, as I slid the blonde hair off the table with a napkin and into the trash.

I walked Laura to her car. We made plans to see each other in a couple of days. We kissed and she drove off, just as my neighbour Shantia pulled up next to me and got out.

"Hey Alex, what are you doing tonight," she asked, standing with the door open. Shantia was in her hospital scrubs. She filled them well, both front and back. "I got the night off and Timothy's with his dad," she said.

"Oh. I don't know," I told her.

"I'm looking forward to taking a bath and opening a bottle of wine," she said. "That's not what I meant." She laughed, embarrassed. "You do murals, right?"

"Yeah, I've done some murals," I said.

"I have an idea for Timothy's room. He likes superheroes," she said. "I'll pay you," she quickly added.

"That sounds fun," I told her. "Just let me know what you have in mind and we can make it happen."

"Oh, I'd love to make it happen," she said, looking for reaction. "Come up for a glass of wine tonight. We can discuss it."

Shantia was a single mom a couple years older than me. I tried keeping things professional, since she seemed vulnerable still from her recent divorce.

"I can't tonight," I told her. "I have to visit... a gallery. How about a daytime during the week? Just let me know what days you're free."

I excused myself and ran up ahead, while she was still gathering her personal effects. "Have a great day off," I said.

Just inside the entrance, Tony the janitor was coming out of the common area with a mop and bucket. There was a bulletin board next to the doors with a calendar on it.

"You need any help, Tony?"

"No, I'm alright," he said. "Are you looking to put yourself on the calendar?"

"I'm thinking about it," I told him. "Sometimes I have some art students that want a private class."

"Great idea. Talk to Kathy." That was the office manager. "She's back on Monday."

Seeing Shantia nearing the entrance, I thanked Tony and hurried upstairs.

One line after another made a picture on my tablet. Step by step. Image by image, stories were told.

Work was what I always did. In-between, life happened. Even with comic book illustrations, the need for using my imagination made it worth my time. The drawings, the designs, they were skills to pay the bills.

Any given workday, interruptions happened.

A call came in.

"Are you Alex Emin?"

"May I ask who's calling?"

"You sign your name *ACE*?"

"Alex Claudiu Emin," I said. "Now how can I help you?"

The guy's name was Wilson Greyfogle. He said he did an audio and video podcast, interviewing local artists. Something called *Dark Matter*. I typed it up real quick as he was talking and found nothing online.

"I'm looking it up now but I don't see nothing," I told him.

"It's not up yet," he said. "I'm still collecting interviews."

He said he wanted to interview *me*. It was free exposure.

"I might be interested in something custom too," he said. My ears perked up. "How long you been drawing," he asked.

"My whole life," I told him. "I've been a professional for seven years now. What do you need?"

"I like artist's early work," he said.

"I have some pieces left from when I started," I told him.

"Do you have pieces older than that," he asked. "Like from when you were young."

"You know, it's a funny story," I told him. "When I started out, I threw out every artwork, every sketchbook, every journal that I ever had."

This was something I was oddly proud of. It excited me to have the opportunity to tell.

Wilson laughed.

"Oh yeah, that's fascinating," he said. "You threw out all your artworks?"

"I threw them down the garbage chute one day," I said.

"Too bad," he said.

"It was an impulse, really. The idea," I confided, "was I didn't want to be remembered for my childhood art."

I couldn't help smiling with a stupid pride. To purge mementos of the past, to me, was power.

"So they're gone, forever, eh," he asked.

My ego took over and went down the road of this story. Give an artist an audience, he'll paint you his soul and lose the sale.

"They were childish exercises really. I'm much better now," I told him. "I have many pieces I can show you. Just tell me what you have in mind."

"Don't you regret throwing those old artworks away," he asked.

"Is this an interview… or a commission," I asked him. He seemed like he was kicking tires and not actually buying.

"I was just curious," he laughed. "But I'll call back later." Then he hung up.

I was left with the dial tone in my ear, trying to shake off the conversation. My mind was playing back nostalgic imprints of those formative scribbles, discarded and lost. My childhood dreams of what I would become felt misaligned with who I was this moment.

But I accepted life moved on.

And I continued with my work in progress.

SEE Gallery was in what used to be the Ottawa courthouse back a couple hundred years ago. Men and women were once hanged next to the tall front steps. Now, the building was full of not-for-profit arts organizations. The entrance to SEE Gallery was through the unkept courtyard to the side, down into a semi-basement.

Once inside, the gallery was modern and dimly-lit. It was the type of gallery that was totally empty on weekdays. The ambient lighting made it seem like each piece was an artifact. During opening nights, much like University galleries, the place would be packed with students and academics. All the other days of the month were like being trapped within a pharaoh's mausoleum.

The shiny hardwood floors looked freshly mopped and smelled of vinegar. The walls of SEE Gallery were empty. If it wasn't for the multiple copies of a twenty page treatise, stacked on a fold-out table at the entrance to the gallery space, I would have thought there wasn't an exhibit this month. Sure enough, there was.

I picked up the saddle-stitched pamphlet and thumbed through it like a comic book. My eyes settled on a random paragraph. Something about one thing "juxtaposed" with another and filled with a lot of convoluted words which explained why what appeared to be an empty art gallery actually wasn't. The dissertation supported the gallery space with inclusivity-suffused contextualizations, while my eyes were juxtaposed with blank walls.

I set the thesis down and looked around. At the far end of the gallery there was something. A pedestal with a one-foot-squared surface standing solemnly. Since there was nothing else in the space, I figured I'd walk over and see what it was all about. As I approached, a stack of glass plates came into focus on the pedestal. They were glued together and the whole stack formed a cube. I bent down to see it. There were 12 slides and each slide had an old frame of film. The sequence was from a pornographic film.

That was all there was to see. I walked toward the offices.

Two ginger twins were revealed through the first open door. They were sitting at tin-legged desks, swamped among stacks of paper. One was the paperwork guy and one was the curator. James St. Denis sat behind the desk ticking away at his keyboard, the computer screen reflected on his black-rimmed glasses. Tim St. Denis leaned next to the slim basement window, clicking with his thumb through a vintage slide projector. The images projected onto the wall vis-à-vis. The thin line of smoke from his cigarette trailed to the outside. His orange-filtered *du Maurier* had about a fingernail left. A long trail of ash stained the silver disposable ashtray.

Nobody greeted me for thirty seconds, although they sensed my presence. This showed me where I stood with them. They must have heard my footsteps.

"What are you guys working on?" I finally broke and asked.

"It's grant season," said James. Tim added, "This exhibit is coming down next week and the next one's going up."

"I'm trying to get a solo show myself," I told them.

"Cool. You got a gallery representing you," asked James.

"That's why I'm here."

"You're still doing paintings," asked Tim.

"Yeah."

"We don't do paintings. You know that," said Tim.

"I know. I'm just putting it out there."

"He can still apply. You never know," said James, turning to Tim.

"Sorry, I didn't mean to dissuade you," said Tim. "It's not us. It's a jury process which decides." That wasn't totally true. They had more say than Tim let on. "SEE is not-for-profit. We have to fulfill our grant quotas," he said.

"It's cool," I said. "I get it."

"Have you been awarded any grants," asked James. "Often having a grant behind you looks better on the application. It might just get you in."

"I tried grants."

"And?"

"I'm still here."

"Well keep trying," said James.

"Success is failing nine times and winning once," said Tim, without shifting his eyes from the slides he was clicking through.

"Have you tried the city commissions," asked James.

"City commissions?"

"Yeah. The city has these opportunities for artists and a lot of money's exchanged. I'll send you a link," he said.

"I'd appreciate that. Thanks. It would sure beat drawing comics," I blurted. I said it to fit into their inner circle. In reality drawing comics was a dream since the time I found a comics bin at a flea market when I was ten.

Tim butted out his cigarette. Smoke escaped through his mouth and nose as he spoke. He said, "Comics are so pedestrian."

His comment hurt me.

"I suppose I did walk in off the street," I told them.

"That's not what it means, Alex."

They didn't explain but I knew. Pedestrian meant comics were for the common people. Fine art for the elite. James and Tim saw themselves as art connoisseurs with clout in the local art world. I saw them as barnacles on a whale.

"Sorry, we have a lot of work today," said James.

And I was simply a fish that couldn't fit in or catch up to a school.

On my way out, I stopped by the bulletin board at the top of the stairs. My business card was still pinned up. I grabbed a flyer of an upcoming exhibit and a pamphlet on how to write grant applications.

The info session was on Bruyerre Street. A dusty high school built in the 1970s, windows cracked open with a hinge. I walked around from the parking lot to the front steps. Each step to the front doors brought back the memories of the oppression that I felt as a teen, with school withholding the life I so badly wanted to start already. Making it past the threshold, the halls were foggy and trampled and full of the clamor of young ghosts.

A greeter with a clipboard was waiting to point me to the second floor. Through the heavy doors, were the stairs. Entering the repurposed classroom, sixteen faces turned in acknowledgment. I sat down at the end of the board table. I had come like everyone else, to find out more. This particular commission was for a project on Wellington Street. The City wanted to cover up graffiti and create inspiring artwork that showed the many cultures along Wellington Street. There were Lebanese (east of Bank Street), Chinese (west of Bank Street), and Little Italy on Preston. The City's budget was $75,000.

The middle-aged presenter went through the specs on an overhead projector. I had to hold in a yawn during his presentation. Afterward, he opened it up to Q&A. The questions disclosed who some of the main candidates were. The first to speak was a married couple who already won a $50,000 commission from the City. Their previous win was a series of cutout tin plaques that were hung on lampposts on Rideau Street. Their designs were inspired by the tapestries of William Morris. Little birds and foliage. Twirly vines and shapely leaves of grass. They introduced themselves as insiders and asked if similar designs to their prior project might be of interest.

"We pay you for the maquette," the grey-haired presenter pointed out. "If you're a finalist, that is."

Another character at the boardroom table was a construction manager. She was taking notes for her boss who won a few commissions 15 years ago. Their business changed but now they were re-considering going back and putting in proposals.

Another person was a 70 year old man with chapped twisted fingers. One digit was missing. Obviously a sculptor.

There was a young mural couple, known as Gal & Clover. They did murals inside and outside restaurants and private residences. Their style was graffiti. We had met at live events and we followed each other on social media.

It was clear I was out of my league when the presenter mentioned one of the requirements was having a Corporation or a Limited Liability Company. I stayed and listened till the end, through the questions and answers. Then I snuck out like a vagabond, talking to no-one.

My car was parked on Dalhousie Street. Across the street was Neruda Gallery, a five hundred square foot space that looked like a tattoo parlor. Jake the owner tended gay bars in Montreal for about a decade. He saved up his tips and moved back to Ottawa to open the gallery. My work was not edgy enough for downtown. A gallery owner has to believe in your work to sell it. If I could not sell Jake on it, he couldn't sell it for me.

At the end of the block, I spotted Dixon tagging a lamppost. He spray painted with a photo reference. He'd stencil a figure and look at the photo to paint the gradients of the subject with enamel paint. His stuff was so good you'd want to tear the steel lamppost out of the ground and carry it home.

Dixon was a few years my senior, always wore a truckers hat and had a mullet hairstyle. He looked like a redneck. His unusual fashion sense was exactly what made him so attractive. He was the type of man that made you say to yourself, *I understand why girls like him*. He wasn't self-conscious.

I squatted down beside him, chatting him up as he rendered the metal post.

"It seems I see your tags everywhere," I told him.

"Did you see my work at Neruda," he asked.

"No, not yet," I confessed.

"Sold out," he said.

His happy child-like demeanor and glaring bright teeth, overshadowed the bump on the bridge of his nose. Searching the details in the shadows under the brim of his hat, his big blue eyes looked into mine as often as they glanced at his work in progress. Those baby blue eyes smiled widely. They had the wide-eyed glare of madness that only great artists are possessed by. I could see my squating reflection in them. My soul encircled in a bright blue cage.

He told me he was moving to Toronto.

"This show is paying for my move," he said.

"What's in Toronto," I asked him.

"A new life," he told me.

"Looks like you outgrew Ottawa," I said.

"We're artists, Alex. You understand. We don't live in this world. We live here," he pointed to his head. "But mostly we live here," he pointed to his heart. "This world," he said spreading his arms to the street, "this outside world is for the squids." He meant the greasers. Dudes with gel in their hair. The grey suits of this government town.

Before going back to my car, I crossed the street to look into Neruda's gallery. It was closed. There were two large paintings in the windows, one on each side of the front door. Squinting through the tinted glass, I could see Dixon's pieces on the walls. Red dots on all of them. Neruda didn't have to try to sell Dixon's pieces. They moved on their own. It was like his goal to move to Toronto manifested his success.

The paintings were brightly-coloured. Realistic, mixed with cartoony, mixed with graffiti. I admired the techniques but also the materials. Many of the paintings were done on wood planks. He even had a few pieces spray painted meticulously on cardboard scraps. I wondered how long the non-archival paint and paper would take to disintegrate. Fifty years? A hundred? Three hundred?

The heat of the sun beat down.

I got my car and went home, playing back what Dixon said. A sold out show. An artist's dream. He was going to cash his cheque and disappear.

Like a soldier without orders that the war was over, I was left behind. Still fighting. For my day of glory.

The side of the building had no signage - just a grey stucco wall that was decaying. I had the panels leaning at home just taking up space so I offered Dave to bolt them to the side of his building, to beautify his big grey wall.

The triptych was 10 feet wide, with two inch gaps between, and five feet tall. Using a leveler, I used two-by-fours along the bottom, to rest the wood panels against the cement wall, and drove in the screws with an electric drill.

When I was done, I called Dave out to take a photo of me in front of the mural. He grinned and laughed constantly. It was his way. He was sincere.

Britannia Gallery was off the beaten path. It was four blocks from the shops on Wellington Street, among apartment buildings and residential houses. It stood alone on the corner, facing Britannia park. Dave was its sole proprietor.

"Looks phenomenal," he said. His breath wafted a peachy aroma in the brisk air.

"Better than this empty wall," I said.

The subject of the mural was a dinner scene between a man and a woman.

"Hopefully, it'll bring some life to this old gallery," he said. Dave's cheeks were nearly always flustered. He laughed after nearly every phrase he said.

"For sure. How long you been here," I asked.

"Twenty-three years," Dave reminisced, breathing out and relaxing his shoulders. His white facial scruff stood up, showing his age. "Time is the math of life, Alex," he said. "And you don't have to be an artist to hate math."

He told me how he had a small printing press, before the gallery. "That was back when they used to make books by hand," he told me. "The book launches turned to exhibits of the illustrations from inside the books. Pretty soon, I sold more art than books. Then I started to offer the framing. And now we're here. Twenty-three years later."

"Cool. Who you showing now," I asked.

"Steve Flyanski," he said.

I looked around at the paintings on the walls. Flyanski's work that had psychedelic colours. The subject matter was surreal.

"Haven't sold one piece," he giggled. "The framing pays the bills," he told me.

"Really," I said.

"Is it too late for you to quit the business, Alex," he asked with a bigger laugh.

It hadn't crossed my mind to ever quit, I thought. The design studios were in the past - smoldering bridges long abandoned. Even if they'd hire me again, I could never accept the regression, despite the consistent salary. I'm too spoiled by freedom. Too much a victim of my pride. The present existed on the tip of my nerves, as I reached and coiled and reached again towards a goal. My new goal was a show. All I was comprised of was this moment. And this goal. History was in the catalogues of memory. Only the path to my future lay ahead.

The landline rang and Dave ran inside. I dusted myself off, rolled up the extension chord, and put the tools in the back of dad's pick-up truck. I took a good look at the triptych, then I went inside.

The space was about 800 squared feet with 16 foot ceilings. Not a bad size for a gallery. Some of the linoleum floor panels were chipped and scratched and the floor was slightly uneven, especially near the pillar in the middle. To the side was a quartered-off section with wall dividers. That's where Dave made frames. The area took up a quarter of the space. The work table was disorganized with hammers, wires, tapes, and adhesives. There was a mess of framing projects leaning in the corner.

Before I headed out, I wanted to relieve myself. Catching his eyes, I mouthed the word "restroom." He pointed to the back, while still on the phone. I opened a door and faced paint buckets, blankets, and a night lamp. A cup and empty bottles were next to the bedding.

"To the left," he yelled. "That's storage."

Staring at the yellow restroom walls, I thought about the few shows I saw at the gallery. They never impressed me. I don't know if it was due to Dave's taste or just what the location drew. I wanted to show my work in all the other galleries, like PJ's, SEE, and Neruda, but they didn't want me. Britannia was a gallery that would probably die to take me but I thought I was too good for it. However, if I didn't get a gallery show now, my alternative was to continue to show in bars and cafes. I had done that for a few years already. If I wanted to be considered as a real artist, graduating to a commercial gallery was a necessity. It meant charging more for my work and more prestige on my resume, even though galleries didn't usually look at resumes. It was about building relationships. It'd be too easy to have a show here. That's why I didn't want to be part of a gallery that would have me as an artist. I thought I'd rather hold out for something better.

My shoulders were slouched as I came out of the restroom. Dave was off the phone. I stopped and stood next to the pillar. I didn't lean on it but its nearness lent support.

"Thanks for coming by," said Dave.

I stood there looking at the ground. My foot lifted in the direction of the door then did an about face mid-air. Dave grinned, with his eyes darting side to side, waiting for my words. The longest five seconds in the world.

Each second escalated louder in my chest. If I didn't say anything now, I'd forever regret it.

"Can… can I have a show," I asked him.

Dave laughed, before he saw I was serious. "I don't have any group shows until Christmas," he said.

"I don't want a group show," I told him. :I want a solo show. Just me… I have a new series."

"I don't know, Alex. This isn't a good time. Business is kinda slow."

"I'll bring people."

My gut turned. Here I was asking Dave for a solo art show at Britannia Gallery and he was turning me down. What I thought was a sure bet was a bust.

"There's a lot going on," he said. But I cut him off.

"Please Dave…" Here I was begging. Dave breathed out a surprised laugh. I tried to cover up my begging. "This is such a perfect fit, Dave," I told him, looking around. "I'll have just the right amount of canvases and I'm working on a couple of big ones that will look great against that wall there," I said pointing. "And… and I have the mural outside too. So it'll be inside and out. It'll be perfect."

"I appreciate that you're excited, Alex, but it's more than that," he said. "What about sales? Promotion."

The sales were a harder guarantee. This is what JP was getting at. Dave was a nice guy but he had to consider business, like everyone else.

"I have a mailing list," I told him.

"There's a lot of hustle in putting on a show," he said.

"I'm prepared," I told him.

"Well, I'd have to see the calendar," he said.

"I'm flexible on the dates," I told him. "But I want it this year. I've been working on this series for over a year already. I just can't wait any longer."

"Alright, alright," he told me, giving in.

"Thank you, Dave," I told him. "You won't regret it." My feet started spinning, to try to get out, before he changed his mind.

"Save your money, Alex," he said, as I was exiting. "These shows don't come cheap."

"I got the show," I told her. It was great to have someone to share the news with.

After my announcement, we made love with soft caresses.

Lying in bed, Laura asked me, "Why do you do what you do?"

"Art, you mean?"

"Yes, art."

I thought about it long and deeply. "I don't know," I said. "I just want to make people feel how the work of great artists make *me* feel."

116

"You were inspired?"

"I was inspired."

And our lips met with a kiss. We fell in and out of sleep, in and out of love. Until the golden purple sky of morning woke us.

. . .

Laura's duplex was in the Hintonburg area, west of centertown. I tidied myself at the door before I rang the bell. Flowers in hand.

The bright blue *Forget Me Nots* with yellow pistils were potted. Apparently, the flowers got their name from a German knight that died trying to pick them for his sweetheart. His last breath called out, "Forget me not."

"I should have asked you to get wine," she said, opening the door.

I asked her if I should go and buy some. She said she had a couple of bottles but wanted to make sure there was enough.

I told her, "I don't drink."

"You don't drink? That's no fun," said a voice from around the corner. Then a stocky twenty year old appeared. "Hi, I'm Joey," he said, extending his hand like he wanted me to kiss it. "Sorry, I'm sweaty," he added "I'm cooking." He kept going. "Ooo, lovely flowers," he said. "And they're already potted. How thoughtful. Lala, you should keep this guy!" He said the last part while he checked me out, bending backward to the side, like he was going under a limbo bar. "Set them down right there and I'll put them in the window later," he added. Then in a puff, he was back in the kitchen.

Laura and I were left looking at each other, smirking. I was unsure what I just witnessed.

"That's my roommate," she said.

"Did he call you Lala," I asked her.

"Yeah. Joey made it up 'cause I was always singing in the shower," she said.

"You shower together," I asked her.

She laughed and smacked me on the shoulder and ran to the kitchen.

Laura prepared a Greek salad with cherry tomatoes, green olives, and feta cheese. Joey made *linguine alle vongole* with spices and hot clams.

"Normally I make this dish on the cheap with clam sauce from a can," he said.

"It's delicious, Joey. I wanted you to make this linguini the way it was meant to be."

"This is what they serve on the coast of Italy," he said. "They get clams from the Mediterranean and they have a lot of this *linguini alle vongole. Vongole* means clams."

"Very cool," I said, encouraging him. The clams were a little tough. I spat out a couple into my napkin. Joey noticed in the corner of his eye.

His enthusiasm dropped a little, as he continued, "In the land-locked cities, *risotto alla parmigiana* is more popular. Pasta with tomato sauce and fresh basil is the most traditional in Italy."

"You outdid yourself, Joey," said Laura. "You're gonna make a fantastic chef. You should come to France once you graduate. That's where all the great chefs are."

"I wanna be in Vegas," Joey said. "That's where North American chefs go. I can see my name in lights now... Joey Provalone..."

"Pink lights for sure," I blurted out.

"I wouldn't have it any other way," he said.

Laura kept going on about the sauce. She didn't have clams with her pasta.

"It's funny, people's obsession with shellfish," I couldn't stop myself from saying. "You know, clams, oysters, and all that. They die when you crack them open. Seconds after they die, they are in your stomach. In a way, you get to kill them with your bare hands. Most times the oysters come cracked open on ice to your table. This is in restaurants. And lobsters... lobsters are boiled to death in front of your eyes."

"Alex," Laura sprang, pleading me to stop.

"No, really," I said. "Isn't it fascinating how you go to a restaurant and anybody who considers himself a man has to have his steak bloody. We're obsessed with hunting. Humans are ravenous savages still. Or at least we have a fascination with tapping into our animal side. We need to simulate like we killed the damn thing. The closer it is to being alive, the wetter our appetite."

Laura clanked her silver fork on her plate and crossed her arms. "Are you grossing us out on purpose, Alex?"

"I'm sorry… *Lala*." I realized in the moment I was subconsciously jealous of her closeness to Joey. "Basically, I'm agreeing with your choice to be a vegetarian, Laura. That's all I'm saying." And I sucked back a wet clam. This time just swallowing it. Joey was pleased.

"I'm actually vegan which means I don't eat any egg products either," said Laura.

"The linguini is rice based," said Joey.

"Is it gluten free," I asked. "Because I'm gluten free." I was messing with him. It was true I did try to eat gluten free but I broke the rules sometimes for convenience.

"It's gluten free, don't worry," Joey assured me. "Boy, you guys are picky eaters. Lala said you are pescatarian. That's why I chose to make you the clams."

"That's true," I said, forgetting to thank him for considering my diet. "As a pescatarian, I mainly eat just fish," I confessed, "unless there's chicken around. Or bacon."

Something else came to mind.

"In Romania, every Christmas they slaughter a pig," I said, making sure Laura and Joey listened. I wasn't just trying to gross them out. I was sharing a memory. They seemed to understand and gave me audience. "I was at my grandparents place. On my father's side," I continued. "Out in the country. Musta been around four years old. I remember they had a big haystack out in front of the house. On the frost covered muddy road. The women were inside the house and I was propped on the stone gate facing the road. The squeals came first. My dad, granddad, and two other neighbourhood men had roped the fattest pig from the sty and were dragging it through the courtyard. They pulled it past my dangling feet, through the gate, and out into the middle of the muddy road. The heat and weight of their boots melted the frost and softened the mud. Even though this was December."

"Wow. You remember all that," asked Joey.

"This is going to end in tragedy," said Laura.

"Yeah. My dad was the youngest of the men. He did the honours. It always surprised me how cruel he could be sometime. I think it was that same Winter or maybe another Summer. He got rid of some stray kittens on the property by putting them in a sack. Out in the field in back of the house, I watched him as he beat that sack against the ground until there was no movement or sounds from the bag."

"Oh my god, Alex," cried Laura.

"It's the country, you know. Even chickens, he'd just snap their necks. Anyway, the idea is you have to puncture the knife through the neck into the heart very slightly. Enough so the heart keeps pumping blood. The pig was hog-tied, as it squealed and bled out every ounce it had onto the road and down the hill. I stood crying the whole time. Musta been ten minutes. Could have been an hour. Who knows. Eventually, the pig stopped moving and they put it on the stack of dried hay and lit it on fire. The idea was to cook it and kill the bacteria."

Laura was upset I was going into such detail and had already gotten up and was listening from the kitchen, clearing her plate into the garbage.

"The point is, I remember crying when my dad cut off the corner of the pig's ear, right from the smoldering haystack. Because the cartilage was soft on the ear, it was basically smoked now. My dad said it was a delicacy. All the hairs were burnt off as I bit into it. I cried the whole time I was eating. But I never forgot the taste and the smell in my nostrils. The women inside took over the slaughter after that. They made all kinds of sausages. There was food for months."

"That's quite a story," said Joey.

Our trio moved to the living room which was lit with aromatic candles. By the time we had dessert and tea, the atmosphere had lightened up. Laura brought out her vegan *crème brule*. She actually asked me beforehand what I wanted for dessert and I told her that was my favorite. It was true and it just so happened to be a

French dessert she knew how to make. She used vanilla custard. Chamomile tea was served in flowery little China cups without ears.

"I have a little gift," I told her, going to the door to get the present out of my messenger bag.

"What gift? What? No," she said, surprised.

As she was unwrapping her gift, I said, "I know you like Betty and Veronica..."

"Oh my god. It's a drawing of me with Betty and Veronica," she said.

"Yeah. In the same style as the comics," I told her.

The illustration was put behind glass, with matting, in a gold frame. Dave prepared it at Britannia.

"Let's see. Oh how cute," said Joey. "It's a drawing of you, between Betty and Veronica, sipping on a root beer float."

Laura hesitated in showing public affection in front of her roommate but gave me a kiss on the cheek.

In her bedroom, she was frigid.

"We shouldn't, Alex. Not with Joey in the other room," she said.

Maybe I didn't read the signals right, once the night wound down. Soon after we took to her room, I started kissing her.

"He's gay. He won't get jealous. We'll be quiet," I told her.

"What are we doing, Alex," she asked.

"Isn't it obvious," I said.

"I don't mean just now, Alex." The look on her face said it all. It was the look that every girlfriend has, at some point or another. "Maybe we should take it slow for a while. Rewind a little," she said.

"Was it the pig story at dinner," I asked. I don't know what compelled me, I thought. Perhaps I felt like a third wheel with Joey around. Now, in intimate quarters, I needed to assure my closeness to her. But it wasn't working.

"It's not that, Alex. I felt we became intimate too quickly. We just moved too fast."

I went into everything too optimistic, I thought, like a fool.

"If you wanna take a break that's totally cool," I said. "That's cool." The fact I rpeated it I knew revealed my discomfort. Confrontations I always hated, since my parent's divorce. "Why don't you think about it and we'll see what we feel," I told her.

"Are you sure you're okay, Alex," she asked, like she wanted to keep talking about it.

"I totally understand you're not happy with everything, Laura, and there's no need to talk about it," I told her. "There were some red flags I saw too but I'm optimistic. I roll with it," I said.

"You're definitely upset, I can see," she said.

"No, really. I respect whatever you want, Laura. We can date other people. It's cool. You think about it and I'll see you in a few weeks, *maybe*. Or a month. Maybe two. It don't matter," I said.

"But I'm leaving in two months," she said, showing disappointment.

"Well then we'll see," I told her.

I played it cool.

Dr. Weissman was a podiatrist who collected art. He chose two pieces from an inventory link I sent him. I brought his bigger painting unwrapped. His fiancé Janis was also on hand. She grinned, excited, as if she had bought the artworks herself.

"What's this," asked Dr. Weissman.

"Your other painting," I said. "Remember? You chose this one as well."

"Oh yeah," he said. I speculated the smaller piece was his fiancé's selection. It was a watercolour of an elephant against a fiery sunrise. The painting came wrapped in styrofoam, a custom practice in the framing business.

Unwrapping it, I explained to him the special museum quality plexiglass I got for it, how it was UV coated, and I went on about how many frames I looked at to choose the right one for the picture. I was competing with the rest of his collection. A Jackie O Warhol, a Dali, and a Hirst, were hanging in the living room, just over his shoulder.

"What do you think?" I had to prod him for a compliment.

"It's good. I like it," he said, a little sour.

"Here's the invoice," I said, handing it to him.

He asked Janis for his chequebook. She brought it. Her and I celebrated the little artwork. She held it in her hands, while Dr. Weissman filled out the cheque. His cufflinks dinged on the glass table, as he leaned over with his pink Brooks Brothers dress shirt. His cologne wafting past me as he moved.

"I thought it'd be bigger," he said. "I thought this horse piece would be bigger. I don't think it's worth one thousand. When I saw it online, it didn't say anywhere that it was this small. A thousand is too much. I'll give you five hundred."

My stomach sunk. Janis showed a mixture of shock and disappointment as well. She set the picture back down on the table. She didn't want to be a part of the confrontation. Her body language indicated that the purchase was out of her control. However way she felt about the piece, in their relationship, Janis lacked the power of the chequebook.

In politics, I once read, you had to be diplomatic. This was true as well in the art world. The client's purse ruled all persuasion.

"M-maybe I didn't list the size of the artwork online," I stuttered.

It was true, I was remembering. Dr. Weissman viewed the elephant piece in a folder on my storage cloud. The file was uploaded from my camera roll and saved as the default "IMG" something. I had no-one to blame but myself for the error.

"I don't wanna say how much I spent on the framing but it was significant," I told him, hoping not to lose the cost of framing. He had me scrambling to save at least a portion of the money I was expecting.

"You can't force me to pay for it," he said. "Really, it's not worth a thousand dollars. To be honest, I don't even want it. It's just too small. I'll give you the thousand for the larger piece but nowhere did it say how small it was so I don't wanna pay for it."

Janis took an extra step away from us. Her eyes liked the piece, whatever size it was. However, her mouth tightened shut. Her hand covered up the shine of her five karat engagement ring. He was snatching my commission away, as much as he was robbing his fiancé of her gift.

"First of all, the larger piece was fifteen hundred. I agreed to round things down to two thousand since you bought two," I told him.

"Now you're trying to make up for it by acting like you did me a favour," he said.

"I can show you the emails," I told him, standing my ground and fighting back with what little leverage I had.

He thought for a while.

"I have an idea. I'll make the cheque out for two thousand, like our original deal, but I need something else done. I bought a painting in Hawaii. It came rolled up. You buy the wood and whatever you need and make it ready to hang. Okay? Deal? I'll show it to you. It's upstairs."

He held out the cheque, before I could agree or disagree. I took a breath and looked at it. The cliché is that doctors have bad handwriting. It's true, his signature was scribbled but the two and the three zeros were very large and clear. I took the cheque, folded it, and tucked it in my pocket.

After looking at the rolled up artwork, Janis asked me if I wanted to eat. She was preparing pasta. She said it was no trouble and I said okay.

The pasta took a few minutes so I asked if I could get some fresh air. I walked out through the tall glass doors onto the second-floor deck in back of the estate. Outside near the pool, Dr. Weissman had a six foot ice cream sculpture by Claes Oldenburg. I also recognized a John Chamberlain work of steel and a Jeff Koons porcelain. All of them were victims to the elements.

The sun was a couple of hours from setting. It spread its glow behind yellow clouds. There was a pasture and a marsh straight ahead, with houses far off on either side. The grass was tall and swaying tenderly. At first nothing else moved but then something brown showed itself. It was a deer. She lit my face with joy then curiousity. I reached for my phone and fumbled for the record button. On the screen, she looked far away. I pinched my fingers to zoom in and saw something that made me stop. She was limping. She was injured. She was hopping on three legs. I watched her carefully. She hopped slowly and stopped and looked around sadly. Then she hopped again. Finally, she escaped among the trees beyond the marshy weeds.

We ate around the kitchen table. The wall TV was on but silent in the background, playing some financial show. Dr. Weismann was absorbed in it. He asked me if I traded stocks. I said no. Janis asked me about my personal life, if I was seeing someone. She had a daughter in her twenties that lived with roommates and sang gigs in local bars.

"So tell me about your parents," asked Dr. Weismann.

"What do you want to know?"

"Are they together," he asked.

"No," I told him.

"Why not?"

"It's complicated," I said.

"It's not complicated. Just say it."

Whenever I had difficult conversations, by default, I went with the waves. In the *Tao Te Ching*, Lao Tzu wrote that the "best man" acted like water. Water is the strongest force on earth but also the most adaptable. It can corrode rock and iron but also move around them. I must have misconceived that I was stronger than I was because I always flowed with the force of powerful currents.

"I grew up with my father and my mother took off," I answered, now red in the face.

"She left you?"

"Well, left kinda. My father and her didn't get along."

"So you don't see your mother?"

"No."

"How long has it been," he asked.

"Sixteen years," I said.

"Sixteen years? That's ridiculous," he said.

"Well, my father would be hurt if I saw her. I think he was in love with her."

"Are you in a relationship with your father? Go see her."

"Leave him be, Harry," Janis said.

"Stay out of it, Janis. He's a grown man. He can answer."

"I gotta take care of my father," I told him.

"Is your father sick," he asked.

"He used to drink," I told him. "He had a tough childhood. Not to mention what he went through to come out of Romania."

"Are you saying you're a martyr, Alex?"

"A martyr? In what way?"

"You're a martyr," he repeated. "You're saying you're burdened by excuses. Poor you."

"N-no. That's not what I'm saying."

I didn't know what I was saying. I was a stranger to emotions I never addressed. The subject of my mother was one I skirted around. With my girlfriends. With my dad.

"You're saying your father is keeping you from seeing your mother. You can't make decisions for yourself, as a man."

Dr. Weissman couldn't understand what I couldn't explain. My only recourse, I felt, was to be blunt and painfully honest.

"If I met my mother it will just open up the drama of the divorce years," I told him. "They were the worst of my life. I'm just afraid of opening that wound again, I guess."

"Why do you keep feeling sorry for yourself, Alex? You're afraid for no reason," he said. "You don't know what your mother is like."

He kept pushing and pushing and I was in a corner.

"Harry was adopted," Janis blurted out.

This stopped the room.

"Shut up Janis," he turned to her, shouting. Dr. Weissman's face was now blood red with anger. "God, Janis. You don't have to tell Alex all my business," he said. "That's my personal business!"

It was a cartoon to see the difference between the two women Eric and I were dating. Ashley was young and tomboyish. Normally, she'd be in tight yoga pants and a sweatshirt, a baseball cap with a horsetail sticking out through the loop in the back. Tonight, her four inch heels flexed up her calves and thighs in a hot pink bodycon dress that barely covered anything. Laura's outfit would take a couple of looks to draw attention. Blue jeans and a silky green blouse. On close inspection, she wore a higher price tag. Her perfume smelled of French vanilla and lilacs. When I complemented her, she said she mixed it herself from a few different brands.

Eric and I bought the tickets and the popcorn, candy, and sodas.

Ashley raved, "This is supposed to be really good." She hung her arms on Eric's shoulder, kissing his neck and kicking her leg in the air.

In an aside to Eric, I said, "Are you sure it was a wise idea letting the girls choose the movie?'

"It don't matter," Eric said. "The movies are for making out anyways." I thought he was joking but that's exactly what he and Ashley did all movie.

Laura and I weren't as impolite to compete with Eric and Ashley so she just leaned into my arm and rested her head on my shoulder. Their affection lead us to appreciate our quiet company much more.

As the opening credits rolled on the screen, my mind began to reel from the internal game I always played when watching movies. I sifted through the main characters, searching for the one who I identified with most. I relinquished my identity and lived through their actions. With books we have some level of control. We can skip ahead and read the ending. With films, we're at the mercy of the flickering lights. The self awareness of sitting in a theatre faded. All that was left were images across my eyes.

Every scene, every line, revealed potential meaning. Every sequence was a meditation on my life. It was an escape I always welcomed. It was an escape I longed to create through my art. I searched within the film's plot anything I could use in my life. Whether a clever quote, a visual composition, or an example of a character I wanted to be like. As much as I loved life, fantasy was always better. Fiction relied on experience. Fiction was the sweet juice from the orange, while the artist at the end of his creation was a squeezed, sapped, and dry shell of himself. The glass half full with art.

In the lobby, after the film, Eric made some excuse about feeling tired, as Ashley stared at him with lust.

"The movie must have triggered something," I whispered to Laura.

"I'm surprised either of them saw anything," she said.

Laura and I took an evening walk along the Ottawa River. The parliament buildings reflected on the water beside us.

She seemed melancholic. A memory forced itself on her mood.

"My grandparents raised me," she said. "Gappa and Gamma. They took over after mom passed away."

"You didn't say she passed away."

"I thought I mentioned. It's what we have in common," she said, reminding me of what I led her to believe. "You lost your mom and were left with your father and I was left with my father and brother. When I lost mom, I lost my best friend."

"You never got close to your father and brother," I asked.

"They offered me a front-office job at the paint factory," she told me. "They were over my shoulder every day. In my personal life too. I hated it. After a summer of being around them, I booked a holiday to Paris and never turned back."

"That's rough," I said. "Sorry you had to go through all that."

"It's hard for me to talk about," she said. She showed me her locket with a photo of her mom inside.

"She's beautiful," I said.

"She's the ideal woman I aspire to be."

Just listening, I tried not to compare her life with instances from mine.

I just hugged her, warmly.

She was in love with a unicorn. Pure white and impossibly rare.

This was a dream she had. She told me about it, lying in bed. Her head on my shoulder.

"I was alone in an empty white cube," she said. "There was a ladder too."

I asked her, "Where did it lead?" She didn't know. It just floated in the middle of the cube. It faded into the clouds.

"What else was there," I asked her.

"Flowers," she said. "There were flowers surrounding the cube. They went all around the outside, like a hedge up to your waist."

"Where does the unicorn fit in," I asked her.

She said, "The unicorn was feeding on the flowers."

"I wonder what it all means," I said.

"Does everything have to mean something," she asked.

"Laura, have you ever been in love," I asked her.

She looked into my eyes, searching left to right. I waited for her to make the first move.

"There was something else," she told me. "There was a storm but it was very far away."

I said, "I'm curious about the unicorn, Laura."

"Alex," she said. "Come on. It's got nothing to do with us."

"Everything means something," I told her. "You just have to read the signs."

"You live in dreams, Alex," she told me. "You have to wake up to the world around."

"Are you Alex Emin," the voice asked.

"Yes," I said.

"You've been dating a Laura Kazan?"

"Who's this," I asked.

"My name is Richard L. Kazan, Esquire." He sounded young but confident. "I'm part owner and attorney with Kazan Paint Company."

I stood up in my seat and smiled, like it was a sales call. I felt surprised and flattered that Laura put in a good word for me. "Is this an endorsement offer," I asked.

"I'm calling to get to know you." The tone changed. "I have some specific questions that I would like to relay back to Mr. Kazan Senior. Do you have a minute?"

"What's your name again?"

"Richard L. Kazan, Esquire," he said.

"Nice to meet you," I said. "What do you want to know?"

He started off asking about my age, then religion. I thought that was odd to get into religion. What next, politics? But he went light with his next question. He asked my profession. I told him I was an artist, of course. I was excited for a second. Talking about art was what I loved.

"What's your yearly income? Last two years," he said.

The income question blurred the reason for the call. It brought my heart back to Cafe Deckuf. The conversation Laura and I had about being a provider.

"If you're serious about dating Mister Kazan's daughter," he said, "then it's important that you're

139

financially stable. If this is something serious and not just a fling. This isn't a fling, is it, Alex?"

"We didn't talk marriage or anything," I told him, "but I wouldn't call it *a fling*."

He went on.

"Would you say you make over one hundred thousand, or *under*," he asked. I could imagine the smart grin on his face.

All I could do was stumble my words. "To a simple artist like me," I told him, "I measure my success by having a fridge that's full."

"You need more than that to have a good life," he laughed.

I felt tough with distance on the phone. I said, "I guess you need money for experiences too, but I didn't think I needed it to *buy* her love."

"I don't want my *sister*… dating *a bum,*" he snapped.

"Oh, you're Laura's brother," I said. I knew it by the name but I wanted *him* to say it.

"Alright, pal. Take it easy," he said. "Let's change the subject. What do your parents do for a living?"

He was talking as if he had a list in front of him.

"It sounds like the same subject to me," I said.

"I'd like to know what you're made of," he told me.

I wanted to say *How about you go fuck yourself* and hang up. It wasn't clear if this conversation would ever make it back to Laura. If it did, I'm sure she'd be pissed at her brother checking up on me like this.

Then it occurred to me his questions were irrelevant. The point of the call was to scare the shit out of me. Maybe he was just being a big brother or maybe this was about more. Like a lone wolf confronted by a bear, I *usually* ran. I was good at that. But this time, my pride was hurt. I stood my ground and fought with words.

"Listen, *Rich*. Whether I'm in the picture or not, I don't think she's coming home," I told him. "She seems to have a pretty good life, overseas."

"*You* listen, *pal*. Let's keep this between us," he told me.

"Thank you for the call," I said.

As I pushed the phone from my ear and thumbed the hang up button, I heard him smugly say, "Have a good day…"

"We like to say grace," he said. "Since you are our guest and all dat. Would you like to do the honors, Laura?"

"I think she'd rather not," I told him.

I managed not to mention anything to Laura about the call from her brother. I desperately wanted to back out of dinner but once I told dad that I was seeing a girl he insisted. Laura was keen to meet dad, as if she was seriously evaluating me for long-term potential.

"You don't believe in God," he asked her.

"No. I'm actually an atheist," she said.

Under his breath, dad said, "What kind of woman doesn't believe in God?"

She heard.

"A modern woman," she said, as if she wasn't as much defending herself but taking a stand. "But please do what you do. I support your beliefs."

Dad gave me a look like *This is who you picked?*

"She's beautiful but not very smart," he said.

I begged him, "Dad, please."

"At least she could be polite in my own house and all dat," he said.

"I'll say it," I told him.

As I said grace, I could feel dad shaking his head in disbelief. I focused my speech on him. I mentioned how thankful I was for his health, what a wonderful father he was, and what a wonderful life he gave me growing up. I thanked him for the meal. My gratitude for a beautiful and smart girlfriend was also expressed.

We served each other and ate in silence for a while, until dad broke the silence with another assault.

"So Laura, do you like children and all dat?"

"Children," she said.

"Yes, little babies. Do you like them," he asked again.

"Who doesn't like babies," she said.

"Have you asked her, Alex?"

"Asked her what?"

"Have you asked her if she wants to have children and all dat?"

"We haven't talked about children," I told him.

"It's a big responsibility," she said. "It's important to have the right partner," she added.

"You're not getting any younger, either of you," he said.

"Dad has been helping me with the art for the show," I said, trying to change the subject. "Just like the old days. Remember. You used to steal things from work. Scrap pieces I could paint on. This time, he built a whole system for making a large canvas with nuts and bolts."

After taking a minute to make sure the coast was clear, Laura said, "He's been very secretive. I'm curious to see the final product."

"Thanks," I said, touching her hand. "Some pieces are good. Some bad. It's been challenging," I told her.

"You're going to do well," she said, looking in my eyes with certainty and blanketing my hand with comfort. I gripped the ends of her fingers, feeling the warmth of her wet palm.

143

There was a subtext in the air. Laura was being encouraging about my art to show to my dad that she cared for his son.

"He got his artistic talent from me," said dad, while Laura kept gazing into my eyes. Dad scooped up a big fork-load of rice and shoved it into his mouth. Through his chewing teeth he added, "No thanks to his whore of a mother."

It was like a needle yanked off a vinyl record. Everything stopped. Including my heart. And especially Laura's.

"That's a terrible way to speak of the dead," said Laura.

I stammered as I squeezed onto her remaining finger. Her other fingers already pulled away.

"Dead? I wish she was dead," he said.

Her hands were now a foot away. Her heart felt like a mile.

"I'd like to talk to you outside for a minute," she said. I excused us and kicked my chair back to stand up. Laura was already sliding the doors to the back yard.

"I will clear the table and all dat," said dad. "Maybe your woman can volunteer to do the dishes later."

He kept pestering and I was pissed. He was acting bitter and defensive, but his breath smelled cool and sweet.

Laura waited on the back porch, turned away with her arms crossed.

"She lives 50 kilometers away," I confessed. Laura didn't move. "My parents divorced when I was ten. Right after we arrived in Canada. It was a mess. Slashed tires. Bricks through car windows. I had to choose. Either her or him. I haven't seen her since."

There was a long silence. Felt like several minutes. Laura looked back at me, into my eyes, as if trying to access the truth from the lies. Her expressions kept changing, from sympathetic, to somber, to sad.

Finally, she asked me, "Can you take me home?"

When we stepped inside the house, dad was putting away something in the cupboard.

Laura went to the bathroom to powder her nose and I told my dad she wasn't feeling well. We had to go.

He said, "Was it my comment about the dishes? She thinks she is too good to do dishes and all dat?"

Laura just stared out the car window the whole ride.

"I can't imagine not wanting to have your mom in your life, Alex," she said.

I said, "I'm sorry. I meant to spare you from the drama and I was ashamed of admitting I came from a dysfunctional family."

"You don't have closure on the past," she said, "and that's a problem."

"I've accepted that's the way it is," I told her.

"Was she a bad woman," she asked.

"To be honest," I said, "I don't know. My memories are faded and what dad said about her is painted with mud."

"I get it that you have family troubles, Alex," she said. "Every family has their own challenges. That's not the issue. The fact that you lied to me is the issue."

"I know I'm not *perfect*," I said. Using the word "perfect," I was trying to be clever. To make her turn against it and maybe see we all have our flaws.

"My grandparents were the only light left in my life, Alex. Those memories on the lake are all I have of my childhood. My heart still lives on that lake. But you, you run away from your history. You focus too much on your work and the future."

"That's all I have," I told her. "My show. Success. Why do you think I do this?"

She shook her head.

"Living in the future is the same as living in the past, Alex. In both instances, you're left totally blind to the present."

She was too far-sighted to indulge me any further. We went back to silence for a stretch.

When she got out of the car, she said, "I want you to know Alex. I understand your situation. I'm just disappointed the way you handled it." She thought for a moment and added, "Our backgrounds are too different anyway."

That last comment confirmed she probably had a conversation with her brother or father but she didn't mention it.

"If we were characters in a book," she said, "maybe we could keep going like this. Maybe things would resolve themselves. The way it's been going, I just don't see how this could end well."

I opened up my hand. She held it.

Her other arm reached for the door.

Laura said, "Good night, *Romeo.*"

Her hand faded from mine. The car door closed me in alone. On the other side of the glass, her silhouette blurred with our distance.

Dreams are funny.

I had a sedan with all sorts of trouble. This was the second time I had to call the mechanic. His voice sounded different. Do I have the right number, I asked. He said yeah but he's the salesman. I was driving, as I was calling, on a wet downward road. Weaving in and out of cars, I was all of a sudden a *drone*, viewing the car from above. It was muggy out. Foggy, and the roads were dirty. The car sped toward a t-junction, amid a procession of traffic.

It escalated into a high speed chase. I realized it was no longer me driving. It was my dad behind the wheel. There was a voiceover telling me he died this way. *A heart attack behind the wheel.* I could imagine his pulse rising from road rage. The temperature had lowered drastically, as his car drove upward along a straight paved road. Uniformed police with navy blue suits were on his tail. I was still in the air, watching it all. I flew in closer, as I saw his car had slowed down and pulled over. There was snow on the ground and light flakes were coming down. I neared the back of the car which was now his familiar pick-up truck. Across the street where he had pulled over, there was a row of about six to eight police cars but the cars were shaped like excavator cabs with those three big rectangular windows. In each cab, you could see a stern blue-jacketed officer. Their coats were decorated with medals and they stood upright. They looked serious and the whole scene felt like some sort of naval funeral procession.

The windows were closed on all the cabs, except for one. In one, there was a young lady. Brunette. She was barely wearing anything. The front window was flung open, with the snowflakes and the cold coming in. Her feet were on the chair and she was cradling her knees, shivering.

I neared the driver's side of my father's truck, like a police officer giving a ticket. His window was open. I leaned my head in close to his. His bitter breath stung my nostrils but I welcomed it. He was out of breath. It felt like I was catching him at time of death. My face was close to his, nearly cheek-to-cheek and eye-to-eye. What he said next, he said without moving his lips. He spoke in neither Romanian nor English. He spoke in the most altruistic spirit I've ever heard from him. *I wish you and this young lady well*, he said. *I want you to be as happy together as you could possibly be.*

And that's when I woke up crying and angry. Angry that he was never willing to just be hopeful like that when he was alive. And crying just because love hurts sometimes.

"You must be Alex. Come in."

We shook hands.

She led the way past the sun beams streaming through the floor to ceiling windows, and then past the counters and the tellers.

Her office wall and door were made of glass. Behind her chair and desk, the thick black blinds were tightly closed. The white walls sandwiched us. The desk had hardly anything on it, as if multiple people shared the office. It was just a meeting room to give appearances. A computer screen and keyboard was in one corner of the desk, a box of tissue behind the monitor, and her business cards were in the other corner nearest me.

"Have a seat and tell me how I can help you," she said.

"I need some financial advice," I told her. "I'm going to be coming into some money soon and I want to be able to manage it, you know."

"How much are you looking to invest," she asked.

"I haven't made it yet so I'm not sure," I said.

"I see. What business are you in," she asked.

"I'm an artist," I told her.

"That's amazing," she said. "What kind of art do you do?" This was a question I got all the time. Professionals were always so impressed I was an artist, in a pity sort of way. Like a child from art class that never grew up.

"Well, I'm an illustrator but I also do fine art," I said.

"That's fascinating."

"Drawing comics is my bread and butter," I told her, "but I'm trying to sell paintings."

"That's so admirable. I can't even draw a circle. That's how bad I am at drawing," she giggled.

"Actually, drawing a circle freehand is not easy at all," I said all too seriously. "The trick is to feather your lines lightly and go nice and slow. It'll never be perfect if you try and draw it all at once. A good artist would anticipate the curves." She didn't need or care for this long-winded explanation. "Anyway," I continued, "I have an art show coming up and several artworks are priced at 10 to 20 thousand dollars."

"Wow. Congratulations. Do you have an RRSP?"

"What's that," I asked.

"They call it a 401K in the US. It's an after-tax saving program for retirement. Has your company every talked to you about that?"

"What company? I'm self-employed."

"Right. There are solo RRSP plans and we can help you with that. Or investing in index funds."

"I need help with my plan. Do you have experience with planning?"

My vagueness confused her.

"We can definitely help you plan your finances. I've been a financial advisor with the Bank of Ottawa for three years and this is my specialty so you're in good hands. Tell me, what's your goal?"

I was like a locomotive entering a tunnel. Everything got dark. My thoughts. My heart.

"All I have left is my art," I said.

"Okay," said the banker.

I was telling her what I wasn't brave enough to tell myself. "When everything is gone," I said, "all I have is me alone with my art. Art is my only constant."

Her eyes shifted side to side, as if looking for a panic button. There was none.

She was trapped. And I was trapped.

My hands prayed between my knees, as my body sat still. Inside, I flailed around, full of emotions, like a kamikaze moth burning with the heat of a lightbulb.

"I want so badly to believe that I can change my fortune," I told the banker finally. "I want to sell a lot of art. I want to get some money in my life. And then things will get easy."

I looked at my reflection on her black computer screen. The banker patted paper on her desk.

"So that's my goal," I said, "to make a lot of money." I grinned as if having all the power in the world. But her and I both knew that I had nothing.

She looked concerned for my emotional well-being.

"Maybe that's asking too much," I thought out loud.

"If you *have* money," she said, "and you want to open a savings account and accrue interest, I'd be happy to help you… sir."

She scrambled for solutions, all the while looking at me as if I was lost. I wasn't sure anymore why I was here or what I was saying.

"I'm stressed," I admitted. The weight of my forehead pulling me down.

"It's alright," she said. "Diamonds are created under pressure." She wanted to touch my hand but she hesitated. She tapped her fingers on the table, keeping her gestures professional. "Let's open up your bank account and see what we can do."

The blue glare of her computer screen lit my face. As her nervous fingers tapped on keys, my eyes got bleary.

"When is your art show, by the way," she asked, while evaluating my *balance*.

As soon as Eric told me, I got real quiet.

"I got a ten thousand dollar commission today," he said. "From some government asshole that works with Ashley. He's got a side hustle. Needs a website."

"Wow. That's lucky," I said.

He said, "Some guys get lucky. Some guys stay broke."

"So you invoiced him already," I asked.

"Invoiced? No. I'm too busy with school," he told me.

"Well then how did you get the deposit?"

"I don't need a deposit."

"Wow, that's brave," I said. "I would never start work without a deposit."

Eric puffed on a joint, while I modeled a piece of clay with my hands.

"By the way, if you come across my weed pipe, let me know," he said. "I don't know where I left it."

"So you're only selling him the concept," I asked.

"Not just the concept, Alex," he said. "A beautiful new design and the best goddamn website that anyone's ever seen."

He showed me on his laptop how he was designing the look of the site, page by page. He explained how it was up to the client to find a programmer to make it functional. Then he went on adjusting the kerning between the letters of each font. He was turning each letter into vector art and nudging it individually.

"Now I see why it costs so much," I told him, as he took another toke of his joint. He laughed at my sarcasm. I didn't want to press too much and give away my envy. Instead, I kept pushing on the modeling clay with my fingers.

It was the dry type that you cook in a conventional oven. My thumbs pressed and pinched the pink clay between my warm palms. The heat made it bend and fold to my whims. More than painting, molding something with my own hands brought me closer to creation. Prometheus and I were thieves. My stolen fire was generated from the heat of my hands. My thumbs and forefingers were having an ancient conversation with the material I held. Out of muck, I was crafting my beautiful monster. My work of art.

"What are you making there," asked Eric. "Looks like an arm."

I stared at it, and told him, "I call it... *Fist of Anger*."

"I might be in trouble and all dat. But he asked for it," he said.

I barely came through the door and this is what greeted me.

"What's goin' on," I asked.

He stood there, rubbing his right hand which was swollen to double the size. Knuckles cracked and bloody. I didn't tell him about the fist I was modeling out of clay this morning. Coincidences happen. If I read too much into them, I feared I'd run insane. So I blinked the thoughts away and listened.

"This guy at work," he told me. "His face ran into my fist and all dat."

There was a double shot glass of vodka next to a half drunk bottle on the coffee table. His drinking was back into the open. Dad downed the glass and immediately poured another.

I convinced him once to attend a meeting of Alcoholics Anonymous. It was held in a church basement. He called them all *a bunch of losers* sitting around on plastic chairs. After, he said to me, "People live. They drink. The drinking is not the problem and all dat. Life is the problem, my son."

"I thought you were going to AA," I said.

"I thought you were off drugs," he said, with a *how dare you* look on his face.

I said, "What are you talking about?"

"You are doing the crack and all dat," he said. "Don't lie to me. I found a pipe in the drive way."

"What? When?"

"After your girlfriend visit."

"Oh, was it a copper pipe," I laughed. "That's Eric's," I realized.

"I don't care who's it is. Just don't do it," he said.

"It's just weed, dad. I smoke it socially," I said.

"I don't want to see you like you were years ago and all dat. You remember I took you to my friend barbecue? I told you to sit down. You just stand up next to me with a blank look on your face. Everybody else was sitting. You were the only one standing. Your hands behind your back. Staring out like a zombie for three hours. Don't tell me you were not on drugs."

I restrained myself from indulging the argument of one flawed character pointing out the mistakes of another.

"Can I have the pipe," I asked.

"Why you want it?"

"To bring it back to Eric."

"I threw it away," he said.

"No you didn't."

"Yes I did."

"You threw it where?"

"I threw it in the field at the back of the house," he said. "You can look for it if you want."

It was lost.

I rolled my eyes.

"What the hell happened to your hand," I asked.

He said, "He was picking on me and all dat. I told you."

"No you didn't."

"You never listen," he said.

He stopped cold. He heard something. Then I heard something too. Motorcycles blasted their mufflers outside.

Dad looked at me. "Are you expecting anybody?"

"No."

We heard the mud room door open. A knock came at the door and two six foot men walked in without waiting for us to answer. They were at least 250 pounds each. They had beards, tattoos, and leather vests and jeans.

The first one said, "Hey Johnny... Just checking up on you."

The second guy said, "How you feelin'?"

Dad told me about this kind of stuff, back in Romania, during communist times. While he was trying to escape, the police would knock on his door unannounced and harass him. They'd hand him his mail, opened.

I said, "Who are you guys?"

The first one with the red beard said, "Who are you?"

"Leave my son out of this," said dad.

"We're just here to see how you're feeling, Johnny boy. Don't make more trouble than is needed."

"Yeah," said the second one, "Don't you think you did enough today?"

"Maybe we should call the police," said dad.

I looked around and saw the shotgun peeking from around the couch.

All smug, like they weren't scared at all, the redhead said, "Go ahead and call 'em, Johnny boy."

I've never been so scared in my life. It felt like something out of a mobster movie, like they came here to kill us. But that kind of stuff couldn't happen in

Canada. I thought we were a peaceful nation made up of peaceful people.

It was self-defense, I thought. And I grabbed the shotgun.

I pumped the action.

The barrel pointed to the bikers.

"Talk into the microphone," I said, like I was inside my own action movie.

My nerves were running wild inside my chest.

The bikers immediately put their hands up and took one step back. In my mind, I saw a bloody mess. Dad stared at me with shock, scared of the consequences. One mistake following another.

"Alex," he said. "Don't do anything you will regret."

"Take it easy eh," they said.

"He was just cleaning it," dad told them. He was trying now to provide me with an alibi.

"Alright John, you crazy son of a bitch. You better take a few days off of work... Okay?" They backed out nice and easy, hands up, back through the mud room door.

Dad called after them, laughing, "You don't want to stay for tea?"

They drove off. Gravel splashing in the driveway.

Dad looked at me and laughed and grabbed the bottle of vodka.

"Please put that away," he said.

He collapsed onto the sofa, weeping. I sat down next to him and put my arm around him. The shotgun in plain view, against the armrest.

"Tell me what happened," I said.

He finally opened up.

"A guy was after my ass at the shop and all dat. A young guy. Around your age. I don't know why he did not pick on somebody his own age and all dat. He thinks if I got an accent I am also stupid. I told him. Do not fuck with me and all dat. If you pick a fight, I will give you fight. He said, 'anytime old man. Just pick the time and place.' I did. Except I did not pick when he was ready. I picked when I was ready."

I brought him a pack of frozen broccoli from the fridge, as he explained. He ignored it and poured himself a glass instead.

"Go on," I said.

"For weeks he has been asking for it. Making fun of my accent and all dat. I warned him. He thought I was playing. He is 20 years younger so I don't take my chances. I waited. Today was the day. We were having our morning smoke break before starting work. He said some shit in front of the guys, as usual, and again with 'anytime, anyplace.' Everybody went inside and I was sitting. He was the last one before me. 'Anytime, John, anytime,' he said. I got up as he went by me and started on him. He did not see it coming. I knocked him down with a couple of punches. He kept coming at me but didn't land nothing. I told him, 'stay down you fuck or I am going beat the living shit out of you.'"

"So that's how you broke your hand," I said.

"When I heard my hand crack, I started with the kicking. Gave him the *boot*, as the Canadian say."

"We gotta take you to the hospital," I said.

"I can't go to the hospital," he said, taking a sip of vodka.

"Why?"

"They told me not to. I didn't tell you something. He's the owner's nephew."

"Who is?"

"The guy."

"You beat up the owner's nephew?"

Dad massaged his hand. "I know. Is bad," he said.

His face soured with another swig of vodka.

Emily called my name from behind the counter.

I leaned to Laura and said, "Have a seat and I'll get our coffees."

"I don't know what I want," she said.

"You notice anything different about me," asked Emily.

Laura watched us, back and forth. Her face was bathed with wry amusement.

Emily looked like she put on some weight but I wouldn't be the one to comment.

She pushed her stomach out and framed it with her hands on top and bottom. "I'm having a baby," she beamed. "Oh, and don't worry, Alex. As I told Laura, the baby's not yours," said Emily, laughing.

My neck made a snapping sound, as I shot a look between the two.

"I come here to study all the time," said Laura.

She reached across the counter to pick a fluff out of Emily's blonde hair.

As we got our order, I pieced together why Laura suggested this café.

We sat down. The next five minutes were silent.

"So… you talked to Emily," I asked.

Laura said, "Why are you having your show?"

"She's got a boyfriend," I said.

"It's not that, Alex. I'm talking about your art exhibit. You built up this dream of yours and you don't even know why."

"Of course I know why," I said, accepting the change of subject. "I'm the artist. It's my dream."

"Can you define it," she asked.

I could have steered against the current, by suggesting a different meeting place, but instead I flowed with the waves into the rocky shoreline.

"Why'd you bring me here," I asked her.

"I want you to be happy," she said.

"Are *you* happy," I asked.

"Of course. I'm living *my* dream," she said. "Is this *your* dream, Alex?"

"I'm making a living with art, I told her. "I figure that's good enough."

"It's definitely wonderful. Not everyone is as determined and hardworking as you," she said. "But what's next?"

"The art show," I told her. "What else?"

She gave me a squinted look like I was short-sighted. She was giving me hints. Like a job interviewer that really wanted me to have the job. I just had to answer everything right. But she wasn't telling me what she wanted to hear. She was an open book with no answers.

"Never mind," she said.

I told her, "Come on. What do you want me to say?"

"As smart as you are, Alex," she scoffed, "you're never going to understand women."

I wanted to hang onto her but my emotions were cross-wired. I couldn't say the right thing.

"That's not my job," I told her. I was getting angry now.

"You're right, Alex, that's not your job," she said. "But it'd be nice if you cared to make an effort."

"I feel I've been trying pretty hard since we met," I told her.

She gave me a look that said *I've been patient.* Then she said, "If you have to try that hard, Alex, maybe it's not meant to be."

This was the end.

My mind was exhausted, distracted, I didn't know what.

"Will you come to my show," I asked, in a last-ditch effort to see her again.

She said, "I'll try, Alex. I'll try. But no promises."

Love is only love in hindsight. That was my working thesis. *How could you know it's love, unless you lose it?* Over the years, I've learned that I'm brave. I'm not afraid to love and lose. With Laura, it became an education. Finally.

I realized a little too late, like everything else in my life, that Laura wasn't jealous of Emily. She wasn't trying to create doubts about my art show either. Her confrontation was her way of asking, "What are we?" What did I want in life? Did I care about her?

The roads were wet. The night was warm. I took a long drive along the Ottawa River. The road was quiet and winding in both directions. The wet pavement at night reflected the break lights of cars in front of me.

Across the median, the white headlights beamed the crucifix.

Outside my apartment windows, night closed its drapes on twilight and only faraway stars remained.

Weeks were spent procrastinating, watching video clips online, reasoning that I was getting inspiration. Now came the time for action. My solo art exhibit was approaching within a week and a half. To meet the deadline and have the artworks dry and ready to hang, my body needed to be forced to act. My mind, however, always ran on parallel tracks to my moving hands.

Experiences with Laura replayed in the back of my eyes. The sweet memories of the start with the tart taste of the finish. Everything inbetween. Our dates were like a row of random books on a shelf. All of them had been read. All that remained were mementos in a scattered timeline. The longer one stayed without a book in their hands, the more endless the road ahead became, as the memories distanced. All that remained was the distraction of the action my hands made.

Mixing colours on my palette took my thoughts to my dad. There was something about certain types of general labourers that made them get a job, do just enough to get a paycheck, and quit on payday. It's much easier to repeat a comfortable cycle than to hang in there for the long haul. Getting drunk and fighting at work was the same as quitting for him.

I didn't have the same vices because I saw the dangers watching him. But there was always the risk. The blood. The little education I had made me neither a labourer nor an academic. I was just a gig-to-gig worker with the family drama of a commoner. Despite the metaphors and philosophies that went into my art, my definition of success was merely having money in the bank.

I worked and re-worked ideas on paper and canvas, with chalk and paint. We're taught something, like tying our shoes or driving. We learn to drive faster and communicate to other drivers better. We master the skill so we don't think about it anymore. We do it naturally. Even masterfully. The thing about artists, however, once we do something masterfully so we don't have to think about it anymore, we continue to think about it.

Every paint stroke carried with it its own meaning. Disconnected symbol after symbol, making up a picture. A colour on the left required its balance on the right. Each character's gesture within each picture had to tell some sort of story, good or bad. The importance was that each composition spoke of something that the viewer could interpret. Good or bad. As long as it can make you feel, react, or think.

The artist's vehicle, like the universe, found itself in motion. Unstoppable, the speed lines flew by. By the third day, I found my groove. I put on some Mozart and painted hungry. The practice of my artworks and their intentions became my solitary focus. The questions, the haunting thoughts were far in the rear and out of view.

I worked in my apartment. Days passed, one after the other. The blue tarp on the living room floor crinkled with the traffic of my feet. Splatters of paint decorated it like a house painter's boots. Muddy, sporadic, and thick. Breaks were only spared for breathing. Within the silhouette of my reflection on the window pane, the night sky looked familiar yet different from when I began a few nights ago.

Wilson Greyfogle called again. "Remember me, I called a few months ago," he said. "I asked you about your art."

"You want a commission," I asked.

"Not exactly. Well, kind of."

"I'm just setting up a show," I told him.

"Maybe I can come to the show and explain better."

"Sure." The more, the merrier, I thought.

He hung up.

My mind was full of adding up the prices. The riches I'd be making.

When Dave asked, "How many pieces will you be having in the show," I told him, "About 30. A couple big ones. Most of them medium to small though."

"That's a lot. Okay. What about pricing," he asked.

"What about pricing," I said.

"I have to get the labels made," he told me. "Give me a list and the prices for each piece," he said.

"What do you recommend?"

"Well, you can price by the square footage," he said. "That would be a good way to do it."

"The big ones might be expensive," I told him.

"So are you saying we're gonna be rich," he asked, giggling.

Dreamers always get their hopes up when pricing artworks for a show. At one hundred dollars per square foot, a nine foot by ten foot canvas would come to around $20,000.

"The idea with painting big canvases," said Dave, "was to sell the little ones. Most people staring at a big painting will feel overwhelmed by the size and price or they just won't be able to fit it in their home. Buying a smaller painting won't feel like such a big commitment in comparison."

"I didn't think of it that way," I told him. "It would be nice to sell a big one. Hell, it'd be nice to sell them all," I said.

"I don't know how bad you need the money, Alex. At least I have the framing business. But we'll sell something… *Hopefully*," he joked.

"Yeah, something has to sell," I said.

"Stay positive," he told me. "They say you should always be ready for success, but brace yourself for failure." Then he laughed, to himself.

Someone somewhere said, you can get discovered anytime. I've never been discovered yet. But I promised myself when I started that I would go into every opportunity always hoping for the highest results. I always tried to dress and act with the hopes that someone would find me. Like Warhol found Basquiat. Like Saatchi found Hirst. The more hope I had, the more it hurt when I was disappointed.

All Quiet On the Western Front, my dad would often quote, when life moments were suspiciously quiet. When the day of a show is quiet, it's a good sign. If the morning and afternoon is tumultuous, it's a bad sign. It means you're not ready.

I walked into Britannia Gallery with neither confidence nor despair. I wore my lucky grey dress pants. The familiar spot of paint still on my leg.

Cedrick provided the ambiance. Lillian switched between playing a harp and a flute in the corner, while

Will played guitar and electric piano. They were happy to play for free. They did it for the "exposure." It was a gesture that I could not appreciate in the moment. I was not mature enough to realize that some people just do things because they're nice.

William said, "We're here because we want to make people feel good. We create music to evoke emotions. Writing is for thinking. And art for seeing." He gestured around to my works, as if thanking me the honour of performing.

People trickled in slowly at first and then pretty soon the gallery was full. Chandri and Gary Frank from the Canterbury Community Centre were the first couple I saw. It must have been getting cold outside. They had their puffy Winter coats on.

"Thanks for coming," I said. I could tell they wouldn't buy anything. They just came to show their support.

PJ and Neruda didn't come but I kept a distant flicker of hope for them to see me in my glory. Why would they give me the satisfaction? They never thought of me unless they saw my face.

Steve Flyanski popped in. He complimented my colour choices.

"I came to see what you did with the space." His work from a few months ago had moved on.

Adam Fraser Davidson came too and he and Steve talked with beers in their hands.

Effie turned my head, wearing a bright red frock. She beamed with pinched cheeks.

"What a surprise," I said.

"I wouldn't miss this for the world," she said. "They are all so beautiful."

I told her she looked great.

The banker came with her husband. Effie got pulled aside in a conversation with Adam. Steve handed the banker his card. In the corner of my eye, Effie excused herself away from Adam. Then she lost herself among the colours of the crowd.

No-one was more excited than my high school friend Tanya. She was a positive chick with a bounce in her step. She loved everything I did. As a law clerk for the government, my life appeared glamourous to her. She made me feel famous in her presence, when the rest of the time I felt like a struggling schmuck.

My father walked in like a tornado, turning and twisting bodies as he broke through the crowd with Gladys on his arm. Gladys was a Chilean lady I hadn't seen in years. They dated after the divorce. She was like a mother to me. He didn't stay with her because she was eight years older. It was something he always regretted. Their history was forever etched in the past. The present was for reminiscences only.

She told me how proud she felt.

"Remember me," a voice asked. "I called a few months ago. And then again last week."

It was Wilson Greyfogle.

He was short and scraggly with oily hair. In his fifties. He had a zipped-up canvas jacket. He began to unzip his jacket slowly and showed me an artwork printed on his t-shirt.

"Do you recognize it," he asked, grinning.

The art on his t-shirt was juvenile yet strangely familiar. I stared for a second. It was mine. It was an ink illustration that I did in high school.

"Remember how you said you threw out your sketchbooks? Well, I bought them at the Stittsville Flea Market five years ago. I have your sketchbooks here in this bag. I wanted to surprise you."

"You surprised me," I admitted. I looked around for witnesses. The crowd was getting larger. Faces looked my way for acknowledgement.

"I just need some illustrations for a book I'm writing. Would you trade for them," he asked.

"Excuse me. Trade for what?"

"Do my illustrations for your sketchbooks."

I had to think quick. This guy seemed crazy.

"So you bought my sketchbooks at a flea market," I asked. And now he wanted to blackmail me for free commissioned work.

"I bet you never thought you'd see them again," he said.

I didn't like being blackmailed to do commissioned work for free.

I said, "Listen buddy, I threw those sketchbooks out because I didn't want them. I don't even know if there's anything worth saving."

In truth, I was curious what he had exactly. But I didn't want to work for free. My concern was that he read my journals. My high school and college journals were part of that purge and I thought I saw a couple of small books in his canvas duffelbag.

Constantin and his mom arrived and were waving me over. Wilson Greyfogle noticed and offered to excuse himself.

"How about I send you scans by email and we can see from there? Okay?"

"Alright," I told him.

Greyfogle scurried away through the crowd, leaving me with a lump in my gut. A camera guy from Channel One showed up. He framed me in front of my centerpiece and prompted me with questions, as I watched Greyfogle aim his finger at me from the doorway. And he made his exit.

"This was a show that I worked really hard on," I said into the camera, distracted.

The reporter peeked from around his lens and said, "Let's do that again." Having a dumb look on my face was acceptable for such interviews but ending a sentence with the words "hard-on" wouldn't quite cut it for the six o'clock news.

Once the camera light went off my face, my smile diminished with it. My back remained a foot away from the wall, standing there like in a police line-up. The chatter of the crowd passed me in waves, like stormy waters. The sounds of conversations rose and dipped, with the sea of people. The spotlights shone on black and navy garments, contrasting the colours of my artworks on the walls.

I stood motionless, like a portrait in a frame.

Person after person walked up to me, like staring at the Mona Lisa. They took photos with me and congratulated me.

Norman, his wife Linda, Susan and other artist friends showed up. It was a full house. My students Diane-Marie and her husband Garry. Kito, my private art student, and his mom Lisa. Dr. Weissman and Janis came too. Everyone was complementary. Dave was being a good gallerist and a good host, replenishing the grapes, cheese, and crackers on the side table, and making sure two bottles of wine were opened and plastic cups were neatly stacked. All that was left for me to do was smile and greet my fans.

Emily came accompanied by a tall dude. Her stomach protruded a few inches more. Dad's neighbour Nick came with his wife and little Sophie. My neighbour Shantia brought her son. With their age in common, the kids were introduced. Neighbours also came and my building manager too. There were very few I didn't recognize. Everyone was here. It was a dream come true.

Joey showed up, without Laura. The void was felt. He answered what I was afraid to ask. He said, "Laura is studying tonight. She wishes you good luck."

Dad was happy and a little tipsy. "I just talked to the Ambassador from the Romanian Embassy," he said. "I can't believe he came to your big show and all dat."

"He was on my newsletter," I said.

Dad pulled out a mickey of vodka from his jacket pocket and snuck a swig. When I reproached him with a look of embarrassment, he said, "I don't drink this shitty wine." Then he dragged Gladys to socialized outside and smoke a cigarette. Constantin's mom joined him even though she didn't smoke. There were a couple of other Romanians too. It was a mini congregation. Of course, my mom was missing. But I imagined her there.

Somewhere past the middle point, Diamond and Katerina made an entrance. Their stilettos pierced the linoleum floor. Stuck. Unstuck. And popped like bubble gum. They drew attention like approaching headlights. Pearls and gold were strung across their cleavage.

Diamond wore a faux leather jacket with a black sequence dress. Katerina had a fur vest with a cheetah print bodycon. It looked like a fox was riding a cheetah.

Eric came with Ashley. He wore an off-the-rack suit that hung on him loosely and she froze her tush in a tight skirt. They floated around while I chatted with other people. She squirmed as he whispered into her neck and pointed to paintings. Dave joined them for a pantomime. Eventually, they made their way to me.

"He what?! That was my lucky pipe," said Eric.

I explained to him the situation. "Dad threw it away. I'm sorry."

He was pissed. He rolled his eyes and scoffed and walked away with Ashley, just as quickly as he appeared.

Those were the highlights.

The crowd trickled down. People said goodbye. What started with firm handshakes at the start of the night ended with warm hugs.

I made sure Lillian and William took home a couple of bottles of wine. People gave them lots of compliments, all throughout the night. Lillian told me how impressed they both were with my art and how everyone had a great time. The thank you and hugs I gave them were from my heart. They loaded up their car and disappeared.

The gallery was nearly empty now. Diamond and Katerina were trailing. I told them, "Stick around."

"Fantastic turnout," Dave said, surfacing from the back.

"You need any help cleaning up?"

"No. It's alright," he told me. "I'll take care of it all tomorrow."

"Any sales," I asked.

"Four small pieces," he said.

I thought, *that's it?* After the gallery's commission, it must be like 400 bucks.

"Who were the buyers," I asked.

"Some lady from the Bank of Ottawa bought that series of three little reindeer," said Dave. "Your buddy Eric also bought a piece. The figure painting."

The banker bought a series. Eric bought a piece too. I couldn't believe it. I turned to look for Eric but he left. The view through the stenciled window showed the parking lot was empty. Just my car remained, like a looming ghost.

Dave said, "The show's up for a month, Alex. We'll get more sales. Don't worry. Just go home. Relax. And congratulations, my friend."

Two high-legged silhouettes materialized out of the muraled backgrounds. They blended in yet they stood out. They came to see the show, emptied their perfume bottles, put on their most glittery miniskirts, and now they needed something else to do for the rest of the night. They thought it was gonna be a much wilder party. A longer lasting thrill. Ten thirty was brunch time for these ladies.

We went back to their place. We cracked open leftover bottles of Prosecco from the show. I fell back onto their shaggy sofa. They danced with their hips to ambient music. Black light highlighted everything like at the club. They did a good job recreating the climate they're used to. Their flowing bodies glowed against the background furniture like fluorescent algae, sexualized.

At one point, Diamond put her head in my lap and started blowing me. From there, the three of us followed through with our natural instincts.

In the middle of the night, dreams woke me and I found myself in the bathroom in front of the mirror.

Somehow, sleeping with Katerina and Diamond seemed like it would be a victory. A consolation prize. They saw the night as a success. But all I could think of was that I only sold four lousy pieces.

Some say that success is a series of failures put into perspective. But what if you're an artist who's not good with perspective?

Making love to two beautiful women, at this point in my life, was just going through the motions. It was a thin patch for outstanding wounds. I thought I was *Dorian Gray* but I've been walking around as his picture.

Those eyes felt nothing but sickness and sadness for the man staring back in the bathroom mirror. My stomach heaved with convulsions. My face contorted red. At midnight, I turned twenty-nine. And although I didn't have the strength to stand up straight this moment, I felt, deep down, eventually I could.

. . .

Only my lamp burnt brightly.

I lay in bed on top of the covers. My clothes were still on.

The sun went down and came up again.

My phone buzzed, unanswered, on the dresser.

I opened my eyes very slowly, every once in a while. Then closed them again. And opened them again, to see the sun streaming through the crack in the drapes. One more day passed me by.

My phone stopped buzzing when the battery died.

The show was on a Thursday, which is a common day for vernissages. It was okay for me to disappear for the weekend. Not many people needed to reach me, since they overwhelmed me with attention already on opening night. Friday, Saturday, and Sunday was mine to quarantine alone.

Actors, singers, dancers call it the *performer's high*. You prepare a long time for your performance, for your show, and you get tons of attention, and flowers, and then it's over. And then it's dead quiet. And then it's just you, the lamp, and the silence. And often it's dark.

The whole performance feels like a failure because everybody's now gone. You made a few bucks but now what? What's next?

When you're building something up, it's something. Then when the show is on, it's a celebration that you lived up to your promise. You delivered. Not only that. You delivered something unique that only you can do. Something as *useless* and *full of feeling* as art. But when the show and the celebration is over, the emptiness comes.

Every year I took the same path of action. Winter, Spring, Summer, and Fall. And every year I descended into the warm seasons with all sorts of ambition and optimism. By the Fall, I was exhausted and beaten, clawing my way up into the motherly arms of a cold thoughtful Winter again. The motion was like a ball that hung in the air at the top of the year and accelerated as it thrust toward the flames of Summer. Then it collided with July and August, almost bursting from the lava heat, bouncing back up toward Christmas.

If I could just make it to January, then I could draft up *a new plan.*

This year was a total loss. Burn everything. Next year will be different, I thought. Next year, *all my dreams* will come true.

I imagined Laura in some old Napoleonic *chambre*, like pictures I've seen of Versailles. Her window overlooking a far-reaching garden with hedges and statues. The light streaming in from outside, as she unpacks her suitcase on her bed. With her thin hands, she takes each item out carefully, placing clothes neatly-folded into drawers. Finally, she gets to the small gold picture frame I gave her. How would she ever know what's in the back?

To prop it on her dresser would remind her of her disappointment: me. The sad thing, she'll never know that behind that cartoon of her with *Betty and Veronica*, there's a touching portrait of her sleeping. Maybe she'll hide it in a drawer. Even if she displays it, the surprise is hidden. Only if it fell from her hands and shattered, then she would inspect the extra page in back of the cartoon.

Hiding that portrait was never done for her. It was done for some audience that doesn't exist. In an apartment move, maybe she sells it at a garage sale, or maybe she keeps it till she dies. Who gets it then? When the frame is cracked and falling apart at the corners and the paper is dry and stained, someone might separate the withered sheets and find my prize. They will wonder what the story was. Maybe they will search me in the catalogues to see if there is any fortune to be made. The dream is that their treasure is a goldmine, like Leonardo's *Salvator Mundi*, found and preserved after hundreds of years.

Maybe the heartache of my lost love will float my drawing up to the surface light of recognition, from this deep dark lake of anonymity.

People are always in motion. A person comes, they conquer you, you draw them, and they leave. Every artist knows this. If you can capture someone on paper or canvas, you have stopped time. That's immortality. The great tragedy is when lovers disappear and only art remains.

I sat in a booth with nylon seats at the end of the restaurant. Whenever I came to *Memories* on Sussex Drive, I got their house coffee. It came in a classic porcelain mug with a slight taper in the middle. Sipping from the sturdy mug between my fingers, it reminded me of high school when my buddies and I drank coffee and smoked cigarettes until sunrise. On this day, however, my emotions numbed my taste buds and the brown liquid from the white ceramic was flavourless.

At the end of the row of booths was the entrance. A lady walked in. She was short with peppered hair. She stopped in the doorway, nervously scanning the diner for a familiar face. Her eyes landed on mine. She smiled at me. I pressed my lips. She walked toward me.

"Hello son." Her cheeks flushed red and a bitter sweet expression shone from her ocean wet eyes.

I greeted her with just, "Hello," scared to say too much.

She jumped up and gave me a hug. She made my hesitations melt. I've hugged girlfriends and friends but family is different. I realized in the moment of the hug that I had no female friends. Like earlier with Laura, if she wanted to be friends, I saw no point to it. From women, I always needed more because I never had enough growing up. Of course, we were each the heroes of our stories. In some cases, martyrs, as Dr. Weissman suggested.

Mom showed herself to be a good person. She was nothing like the picture my father painted of her. Instead, she was tiny and sweet and honest.

I talked to mom without emotion. I was afraid to let my guard down. She wanted to reach out across the table to hold my hand but she couldn't at first until eventually she begged me with her open palms together. Like reaching for manna from god.

I felt so powerful but so humbled and loved. Reaching out, cupping her hands, holding each other's hands together across the table.

She wanted to hear about me so mostly *I* spoke. She asked me about all the things she missed.

As she listened, tears rolled down her face and into her mouth.

I told her stories. I told her my life. Years were condensed into minutes. Months into seconds. And days got overlooked altogether.

Time flew.

She swallowed her tears, as they reached her lips, then her chin. And she smiled warmly.

When we were all done, she insisted she pay, like a good mom that missed out on so many treats.

On our way out together, I finally asked her what she'd been doing all these years. She told me she cleaned windows for a living.

"I clean windows for skyscrapers," she said. "I'm the best in my profession. I run my own company. We get booked in Montreal, New York, Chicago, London. I travel to Dubai."

She'd been to the top of the world, she told me. That made me happy. She could soar. It was a marvel, all the while, *she* was the fearless one.

I wondered if this meeting was just a dream.

The way it went was nothing like I dreaded. No matter how good my imagination, I was unable to create a person as they truly are. Reality could have become a nightmare, sure, but only if you lost control of your emotions. Once I crossed the bridge of expectations, only the experience and precious time remained.

When we walked outside, she introduced me to her husband Francois who was waiting in front smoking a cigarette. Tears rolled down his sunburnt face.

He didn't say much except, "Your mom told me about you for all the time I knew her."

I walked them to their car.

We said goodbye.

Francois said, "Never leave her life again. Promise."

And I promised.

My shoes rubbed on the carpet, as I entered. Dad was napping on the couch with a cop show playing on TV in the background. I sat on the arm of the couch, glancing at the TV for a few minutes but I didn't pay any attention to the plot. On the floor, dad's shotgun wrapped in canvas caught my eye.

Next thing I knew, I was unraveling it.

The next thing after that, I was holding the shotgun and checking if there was a live cartridge in the chamber.

When I stared over the railing of my fifteenth floor balcony, as a child, I always felt a magnetic pull over the edge. My head wanted to drag my body over. Nausea would overcome me and I'd get a flash of myself spiraling past the lower stories, my little clothes flapping with the speed of falling. My eyes would blur with vertigo.

The only way to avoid the deadly draw was distancing myself from bannisters. But I thought, if I avoided heights and precipices, I'd be living life too carefully. Life was meant to be lived dangerously. So every now and again, I'd inch toward that edge and take a peek into the maddening pull.

This was one of those times when the depths beckoned. Staring over the balcony as a kid was the same as peering into the barrel of this shotgun. Both offered the same dangers. The same end.

I wasted a year and a half of my life, I thought, making art for my solo show. Wasted all kinds of money on supplies. Wasted hundreds of hours that could have been better spent. Worst of all, I invested my heart into the hope that somehow my life would change on the other side of this damn show. The compliments, they didn't matter now. My friends were the same, my family was the same, my income didn't change. My life was like a ghost car, speeding down a desert highway that would eventually end but I didn't know when. All I could do was now and again look out the window and enjoy the landscape. This imaginary desert looked like a muddy mess to me. Nothing to write home about.

Laura was gone. I could fuck around and have flings but I couldn't maintain a relationship. I've been freelancing women like I did my art gigs. Short term thrills with no long term goals in mind. Maybe only *jobbers* could settle down, get married, have kids, a house, the dream. Working nine to five and living five till midnight.

I knew what this was. The feeling was real. It had a steel casing and down the barrel of it was a bullet. Constanin and I talked about our high school friend Chris. With one swift move, he rid of his sorrows but also his joys. I resolved that man's strength was measured by his willingness to live at any cost. Even through pain. Chris had his own particular limit. This was mine.

The trigger sirened the flex of my finger.

"John! John! I need your help," somebody called. The commotion came from the mud room. My dark thoughts, like a painted-over painting, wiped away.

Dad was awake. His neighbour Nick was in the dining room holding his six year old daughter Sophie in his arms.

I tucked the shotgun back where it belonged.

"My little girl banged up her leg real bad," said Nick. "My car won't start. The damned thing. Can you drive us to the hospital?"

Dad coughed a few times and said, "You got it, neighbour. Let me just put on my jacket and all dat."

As he was getting dressed, he asked me, "Alex. Can you come with us and do the driving?" Embarrassed, he added, "I'm drunk."

The car hazards were blinking. I honked repeatedly as I wove in and out of traffic. Dad was in the passenger seat, while Nick had his daughter Sophie's bloody leg wrapped up in the back seat. She was crying.

I dropped them off in front of the emergency room and went to park. There was a small sketchbook in the door frame. I tucked it in the back pocket of my jeans and walked inside. They were still trying to get Sophie seen by a doctor.

"Any news?"

"They'll see her soon," said Nick.

"Come on. Can we get some service," dad demanded, loudly.

There were five other people in the waiting room. They created low whispers and moans of discomfort. A court show trebled from the TV on the wall. Behind me, clicks from the hands of the round clock were heard, like a steady pulse.

"They're short staffed," said Nick.

"This is ridiculous," said dad.

"It's okay. They're gonna see her soon," I said.

"It's not okay," said dad, so everyone could hear. "This is bullshit. We pay taxes for this hospital. And all dat. For what? To wait? We demand some damn service."

One of the two nurses said, "Let's bring her in the back and get her checked in." This was the staff's way to get my dad to calm down.

The blow up exhausted him. Dad's eyelids dropped and he looked behind him for a seat. Seeing him slouch back into a plastic waiting chair, I realized he was basically sleepwalking this whole time. He looked tired, hungover, with bags under his eyes. His hair was a mess and he was unshaven. He always had this very soft scruff. Like taming a lion, I reached over and pet his jaw, feeling his white stubble.

I took my little sketchbook out from my back pocket. It had a leather cover and was about five by seven inches with a pen clipped to the spine. I cracked it open to an empty page. My archival pen hovered above the handmade pulp and glue. Dad's green eyes looked up at me. His mouth, under his mustache, stretched into a glimmer of a grin.

"What made you escape Romania," I asked him, as I began to draw. "From the beginning," I added. "I never heard you tell me from the beginning."

He looked at me for a few seconds, thinking if he had the energy. He saw me sketching. When given audience, exhaustion could be put aside.

"Everybody wanted to leave," he started. "I wasn't the first. A friend and I tried to get a permit to go to the Middle East. Driving a truck. We had to pay. It was a lot of money for the time. At least two months paycheck. I went to the bank and got a cheque made. I gave it to official in a special department. He was in charge of giving the permit."

"Was it like a bribe," I asked.

"Yes. Basically, it was a bribe. But other people paid more so they got the permit. I asked for the money back. He kept the money. He said, the money was just for him to *look into it*."

"So he was doing you a *favour*…"

"Yes. Just for the 'chance.' But I had proof from the bank because I wrote him a cheque. I said, I'm going to take him to court if he doesn't give me back the cheque. I was pissed."

The passion of his memory seemed to awaken him. His eyes got big.

"So he paid you back," I asked.

"Yes," he said.

"So then what happened?"

"So then I went to the border."

"With who?"

"With a couple I knew. Man and woman. They knew the way."

"But what about the Canadian embassy? I thought you had a connection."

As I was observing to draw his neck, I noticed his flannel shirt was one button off. His gold chain and Orthodox cross shone from his open neck collar.

"They just told me they could only help me if I was out of Romania and all dat. I went to the Canadian embassy in Bucharest but dat was after prison."

"Okay. So that was after you got caught the first time?"

"Yes. We were out there for three, four, days. It rained heavy the whole time. We crossed a small river. Maybe 20 feet wide. Water up to my neck. There was supposed to be a grain factory. We knew that if we were close to the grain factory, the border would be close. It was dark. When it rains, it's extra dark outside. You can't see nothing. You don't have the light of the moon."

"Because of the clouds."

"Yes. Because of the clouds. And we couldn't hear the machinery of the grain factory. The rain pouring was loud. We thought in the morning we could see better so we went to sleep."

"Where?"

"Just a field of wheat. But in the morning, we got woken with screaming. 'Traitors! Traitors!' A plowman found us and started screaming to the border patrolmen and all dat. We could see the border. We were less than a hundred yards away. The patrolman fired several rounds in the air. We stood up with our hands up. Romania was known as the bloodiest border in Europe during that time. There was a reason. They can beat you in interrogation, you can get killed in jail, and they shoot you at the border. They were trigger happy. We were caught. Better caught than dead."

He paused, as a couple of hospital staff rushed by with a gurney. We watched them calmly, without comment. He turned back, glanced at my progressing drawing upside down, and continued. "They took us into custody and put us in jail. We had trial too. I got seven months. But I spent seven months minus two weeks. Ceauşescu passed a bill to release prisoners with short terms who were not murderers. Anybody under two years. Something like dat. So I was out two weeks early."

"Not much of a difference. Did you try again right away?"

"I had no choice. Ceausescu took away my citizenship."

"Really? So you couldn't work or make a living?"

"Yes. I could not do anything. They let me back in the country and all dat but I had no rights. I went again."

"With who?"

"A friend of the family."

"Another guy?"

"Yes. But his girlfriend turned us in."

"Really?"

I was in heaven, drawing and listening to him.

From as young as I've ever been, he told me bedtime stories. I'd be tucked in bed and he'd play with my hair. His warmth on the edge of the bed. His voice like calligraphy, scrawled behind my eyelids. His tales spanned a thousand and one nights, till I was too old, till he was too impatient, and until my addiction to the power of imagination was secured.

The tales he weaved back then were things he read, mixed with things from his life. He told tales of *Zmeus*. In Romanian fairy tales, a Zmeu is a powerful dragon. They can assume human form. They can be suitors and lovers to women. I see now, that's how he saw himself. A strong and capable force and a seducer.

I believed everything.

"Her brother was a policeman. My friend gave her *pulă* the night before and told her everything. In the morning, she went straight to her brother."

I squinted to get a better look at him, and outlined his profile. He continued.

"We had a hotel room in Cluj. Ready to leave the next day. Police woke us banging on the door. Took us in for questioning. They kept asking, 'Are you planning to cross the border?' I said, Are you crazy? I'm in Cluj. Over a hundred miles from the border. Not like I'm in Arad or Timişoara. I'm in a hotel in Cluj."

"Did your friend say the same thing or he confessed?"

"They had to let us go. They had no proof. But they kept us almost a full day. After that, I went with the guy's wife."

"But she turned you in."

"Not his girlfriend but *his wife*. Oh she was a tough lady. Really had *sânge în pisdă.*"

One of those determined ladies.

"We were a few days in the forests. Getting close to the border. Hiding. We tried to stay off the paths. If someone came, we could hide. We were close one night but got tired. I said let's just sleep and we'll see where we are in the morning. She was eager. In the morning, it was foggy. We walked into a little town across the border. Everybody spoke Romanian. *Bunâ ziua! Bunâ ziua!* Felt good. Everybody was congratulating us. They took us into a bar. They fed us. The town sheriff was there. It was a small town so he was like the mayor and sheriff in one…"

"Kind of like you, on your block," I interrupted, joking.

"I'm just the mayor," he laughed.

"Sorry. Go on," I said.

"The sheriff, he got pissed drunk. At night, he took us to his house. We carried him. We slept at his house.

In the morning, he served us breakfast and took us to Interpol."

"You couldn't run or something?"

"Run where?"

"I guess, they had to process you. Did you have any letter with you from the Canadian embassy or anything like a promise?"

"I had my revoked passport. That's about it. My birth certificate. Interpol interrogated us separately. I got split with her. They had to put us in jail for three weeks. That was the penalty we had to serve for crossing the border illegally."

"You told me once that the prison in Yugoslavia was the worst."

"No. This prison was a breeze. The Romanian one was bad. Yugoslavia was easy. Wake up when I want. Three meals a day. They just let us roam and we had to come back at night. We could work too. Sometimes the construction companies were short of men so they came and asked if they could get some prisoners to volunteer. You didn't have to but I had nothing to do so I say why not."

"Then they released you and you went to the Canadian embassy?"

"They put me up first at the hotel in Belgrade."

"They who?"

"The United Nations."

He spoke mostly without moving his body. He sloped in the plastic chair, arms outstretched, like he was carrying the aisle of chairs on his back. His right hand reached up to comb his mustache with his yellow thumb and forefinger, just as I was rendering that part. He either needed a cigarette or was thirsty. I palmed my sketchbook and got up to bring him some water in a paper cup. He drank and I continued sketching.

"The United Nations…" I said.

"Yes. They put me up at a hotel called Astoria with the same room that you and your mother came to. I asked for a room with three beds."

The three beds was an indication of their relationship at the time. We all wanted the family to come together then. I shifted my mind to happier recollections.

"I remember taking the train," I said, "and seeing you for the first time."

This was a memory that didn't need to be spoken. Like a spell from a book that unleashes emotions, we cherished the memory in silence. I hung half my body out the window of the moving train, pulling into the station. He grabbed me, fearing that I'd fall. Most of my life, he was the strong protector. Seeing him brittle now, like a leaf in the Autumn breeze, I was realizing finally that his strength was transferring. From one man burdened by many seasons to a man in the thawing Spring of his life.

"You and your mother had to renounce your citizenship too. At the border, you were landed immigrants. You could not go back and you had no visa forward. But somehow United Nations arranged everything."

"Belgrade was the best time of my life," I said. "No school. Free movies. All the ice cream I could eat."

"And later that year we were in Canada," he said.

"There's not a day goes by that I'm not thankful to have grown up in this country," I told him.

"Canada is wonderful," he agreed.

I was drawing the whole time he spoke and now it was finished. What I wanted to tell my father was how I loved him. In this moment, I ceased to judge him on his sins but instead on his achievements. It meant so much to me that he took a risk and made the sacrifice, to bring my willing and sweet mother and me to Canada. Now, when I imagined that unicoloured flag, I saw colours of the rainbow in it, like seeing light reflections through a salty tear hanging to an eyelash. I turned my sketchbook around to reveal my drawing.

His face energized with life and happiness. The picture on the paper was his portrait. Pen and ink, capturing the light coming in.

Presenting him with my picture reminded me of when he was the bravest man I knew. His recollections made him brave again because I knew them to be true.

And again here I was the genuine child, thanking his fairytale with a show of talent that only genes could create.

"Hold on," I said and got up and walked over to the nurses' station.

I brought back a nurse with a medical kit.

"I heard you hurt your hand," she said.

"I don't want to register," said dad.

"You don't have to. Let's see it."

The nurse inspected his hand. The back of it was purple with a bump poking up.

"I tried to push down the bone," he said.

"Oh boy. You really should have had this looked at earlier," she said.

She applied some disinfectant first and then took out some white bandages from her kit and wrapped his hand tight. "Take this splint too," she said. "It was left from our old inventory so it won't be missed."

Dad thanked her.

"Thank your son," she said. "He put in a good word for you. Next time, just be a little patient. Let us do our job eh. We'll get around to everybody."

"I understand," he said. "You are doing your best… and all dat."

Then he slouched back in the plastic chair, feeling sleepy.

Nick came out a minute later.

"How's Sophie," I asked.

"They got her bandaged up," he said. "We're almost finished."

Months went by since I last saw Dave. After my exhibit, I collected most of the artworks that didn't sell. But I left a couple behind at the gallery. The idea was for Dave to display them on the wall or stack them in the corner. If anyone came by and something caught their eye, maybe we'd make an extra sale. It's basically consignment. If I didn't get a call, it meant they didn't sell. I didn't get a call. I wasn't eager to take them back because then I'd have to store them so I left the two pieces behind for too long. I kept thinking about them but dreaded calling.

Eventually, the gallery called me. But it wasn't Dave on the phone. It was someone else. They said, "Come pick them up." I drove right over.

Britannia Gallery was gutted. It looked like there were no shows through the Winter. The linoleum floors, when I walked in, were dusty. Dave's framing setup in the corner was nearly entirely looted. Two gentlemen I never met before were carrying scraps and moving them about. Dave was nowhere.

"Which ones are yours," one of them asked.

I pointed out two paintings leaning on the wall.

"What's going on here," I asked.

"We're calling artists, making sure they get their things."

"Yeah but where's Dave," I asked.

"You haven't heard," said the one with grey hair and balding.

"He's in rehab," said the other one with thick rimmed glasses.

"Rehab?" I had questions. "Why is he in rehab?"

"He was sleeping here. Here at the gallery. In the back." He pointed to the storage room across from the bathroom.

"He took the divorce pretty bad and started drinking."

I didn't know anything about Dave's personal life. This was all news.

"He was living out of the gallery for months," said the second guy. "Sleeping in the storage room in the back. You didn't notice?"

"He's out in Brockville," said the bald guy. "You should call him."

I didn't want to tell them that we weren't that close. The one with the glasses gave me his number.

"Call him."

"Okay."

Later that day, when I went for groceries near St. Laurent, I pulled up next to the black locomotive outside the Science and Technology Museum. I walked up to the monolith, remembering how I used to skip class with my high school girlfriend and climb on top and lay there kissing and charting our lives.

It was a good time to call Dave.

A nurse put me on hold to go bring Dave to the phone. He answered in good spirits, with his usual giggles.

"Nice of you to call," he said. Not embarrassed in any way by his predicament. Just happy and sounding normal.

"I was by the gallery today. Picked up my work," I told him.

"That's good. How are things with you?"

"Everything's good," I said. "How are *you* feeling?"

He explained how his wife kicked him out. He fell off the wagon and now he was in rehab to get his drinking under control.

"How long you gonna be there?"

"A few weeks. Maybe longer. Not sure yet. However long it takes."

It was strange to me to imagine. I read about some artists who went mad, like Van Gogh. To be institutionalized seemed like the end of the road. To lose your mind, as an artist, is to lose your tool. But this wasn't an institution, Dave assured me.

"It's a relaxing facility and very casual," he said.

"Did they give you fuzzy slippers," I asked him.

He laughed for a while. "They're regular slippers, Alex."

"I'm sorry," I said, banging my head with my palm. "How about the gallery? Are you going to reopen?"

"I think it's done," he said. "I've had it long enough."

"But what're you gonna do instead," I asked him.

"Time to retire," he said.

We hung up, soon after that.

I faced him, a foot from his table.

"Hello JP." He seemed to welcome the distraction.

"I'm doing alright," I told him. "Trying to sell a piece here and there. How's it going with you?"

He already had the script for what he wanted to say.

"This rotten fucking town is lousy." People 15 feet away could hear him.

"Wow. Okay. Why don't you leave," I said.

It was good I booked the Ottawa Art Fair months ago. I had leftover pieces to unload from the Britannia show. Several paintings hung on metal grids, I had a portfolio case with illustrations, and copies of my comic book commissions in a bin. JP's booth was double mine, with paintings on the wall, a giant banner, and stacks of 32x48 inch paintings leaning on the side.

"You're fucking lucky, man. You don't own shit."

"What do you mean?"

"I got a mortgage that'll choke a horse," he said. Then he went on about the noise complaints and how his neighbours were suing him. "But fuck 'em. I'll buy something smaller out in Almonte. There I can dominate."

I was always in the orbit of his drama. An uncredited bit player. Like Napoleon exiled to Elba, there was no desire in me as a soldier to follow him. Ambition and success had run its course and spat him out. I thought, *karma*.

"You know, you were kind of a jerk to me," I said. This was my opportunity, to tell him how I really felt, to feel the breeze in my hair with the lift of the seesaw.

"When I asked you for the solo art show. A few months ago," I said.

He looked confused.

"You never asked me for no fucking show."

I ignored him. I was already rolling. I said, "Maybe I'm never gonna be as successful as you. Or sell millions of dollars in paintings. But good and easy, I'm gonna make it. I'm getting the hang of this thing. I found another gallery to show my work, you know…"

"Oh, good for you," he said, "'cause I was tired of your shit not selling in mine."

"I sold six pieces during the show and two more today."

"I see the fucking prices, Alex. They're all under five hundred bucks," he pointed out.

He towered over me a few inches, gripping a palette knife in his hand. The angle of it revealed my reflection. I looked pixelated like a Chuck Close painting, zoomed in. My appearance was cool and metallic, in colours and delight. We stood as men in confrontation, two feet cross.

"You're a real *asshole*," I said, pushing my chest out. People were looking. I was burning bridges but I didn't care. I was unleashing all the built up anger. Some of it had nothing to do with JP. But some of it did.

"Look at you, man. You grew some fucking balls," he said, laughing. "You think you're a big boy now, 'cause you sold a few worthless paintings."

"You know, you told me I don't have it," I said, "but I do. It's not just about selling. It's about having integrity. And if I fail, sure. I try to learn. And I keep going."

He said, "You really *are* a dumbass."

I wanted to leave then. But I stayed. To fight. "No, JP. You're wrong. You're not wrong about everything. Networking is good. But you're wrong about this. You got *flown* to the top of the mountain but I'm climbing still. The climb is more rewarding. And when I peak it'll be *sweet*. And coming down will be a breath of fresh air."

For JP, coming down was hell, I could tell. My sheer existence mocked him, through and through.

I left him there. My knees and body shaking with adrenaline.

By the time I marched to Norman's booth, the jitters left and I was laughing to myself.

My friend asked, "What's so funny?"

"Nothing," I said. For a minute I felt guilty for feeling joy from an ignorant asshole's misery. There was pride though, that I stood up for myself.

Norman had a decent day. He broke even. I was able to be happy for him. We chatted about his wood sculptures and how his online woodworking courses were doing. He had started an online platform. He asked me to contribute a course on painting. We'd split the profits 50/50.

I took down my pieces and packed up my art. In the last hour, I sold another painting. I felt good.

Eric was helpful taping flyers to lamp posts around the theatre and shops. I thanked him by treating him to a poutine from a chip wagon, for lunch. We stooped on a cement barrier, poking our white plastic forks into small paper boxes. Trying to ignore the smell of pigeon crap under the thawing snow, I savoured the cheese curds and gravy and fresh cut fries on my tongue. Around us, the birds reappeared, singing.

"So how many signups you have so far," he asked.

"I have nine students so far. A few of them I poached from the community center. Now I get to sleep in on Saturdays and classes are just downstairs in the common area of my building. I talked to the manager and added myself to the calendar."

"Man, you're constantly selling yourself," said Eric.

"It's the lifestyle of the hustle," I told him. "Between the comic commissions, the art classes, and selling paintings at art fairs, I'm making this thing work. I'm in business for myself," I said.

"Sounds like a lot," said Eric. I wasn't sure if he was overwhelmed that he'd have to do it himself once he graduated, or if he was impressed.

I kept going.

"You remember Dixon," I asked him. "The street artist. Moved to Toronto. Well, he texted me to come down for a group show."

"I thought you only wanted solo shows," said Eric.

"Sure, in Ottawa, yeah. But you gotta break in somehow. Toronto's a bigger market."

"The website's almost finished," Eric said.

"Right. I was going to ask. Have you invoiced finally?"

"No, not yet," he said. "I've been so busy with getting ready for graduation in a couple of months. This will be a great piece for my portfolio though."

I didn't want to tell him that portfolios don't matter much, once your career has started. Networking connections is where the business is at.

"How's your dad doing," asked Eric.

"I haven't seen him much lately," I told him.

"Don't you still have your studio there," he asked.

"Yeah, but I'm taking a break." And that's all I said.

In AA, they say you shouldn't enable alcoholics. So I gave my dad some space. Eric understood. I told him about dad's drinking in the past. He didn't press the subject any further.

After that, I changed the topic to his girlfriend. Immediately, I regretted it. He started telling me about how some nights when he was asleep, he'd wake up to find Ashley riding him.

"Holy shit. That's too much info," I told him.

"What can I say? She loves me," he said.

Effie was working. She flashed me a smile, as I placed my red basket with art supplies on the counter.

She said, "I see you got your cart full."

"I need a lot of art supplies," I laughed. "I have this deal where students can either get their own supplies or for twenty-five bucks, I can buy them for them. I been doing the rounds of the dollar stores and thought I'd stop by Malick's."

"Interesting," she said, and smiled.

"Your hair colour is different," I told her.

She liked that.

"It's been a while since you seen it," she said.

"The green really works well with your brown eyes," I said.

She blushed while she scanned my items.

"Is it possible to put up this flyer on your bulletin board," I showed her.

"Oh neat. Sure. It has to be approved by the manager," she said, "but it won't be a problem. I'll make sure you get the stamp of approval. Just leave it with me."

It's been a few months since I dated. I couldn't tell if she was flirting. She was making eyes but I was too rusty with my pickup lines to make a move.

"So you have an art school now," she asked.

"Yeah, I started my own. Registered and everything." A middle aged blonde lady lined up in the checkout queue behind me.

"That's pretty cool. Congratulations," said Effie.

"Thanks. And by the way…"

"I got you," she said. "Teacher's discount already added." She winked and then got shy.

This was my opening to ask her out.

I didn't take it.

I was afraid I might fail again. Afraid of the effort it might take to make it work. Afraid if it did work, where it might lead.

We stood there awkwardly while she processed my payment and handed me my bag of art supplies.

"Good luck with your classes," she said. "And I'll make sure to get your flyer on the bulletin board."

I thanked her and wished her a good shift at work, on my way out.

Crossing the parking lot was in slow motion. My thoughts a mile a minute.

I stopped.

In the grander scale of things, my life in this moment was all in one movement. I faced rejection before, in business. In love too, there was no sure thing. If I didn't give up with art, I thought, there was no good reason to give up on love.

I saw myself from above. A spec among cars, in a parking lot. To pivot for a second, to turn back and take action, wasn't going to halt the wheels in revolution. If anything, I reasoned, I'd be adding fuel.

By natural propulsion, my body spun around. Took steps toward the entrance.

When Effie heard the chimes of the front door and saw me back again, she shook a bit. She looked around the counter, wondering if she forgot my receipt. The customer in line watched us with anticipation.

I walked up to the counter with my rusty heart affecting my voice.

"Would you like to see my art sometime," I asked her.

Effie's eyes bloomed with life. Her cheeks became shiny like apples, rising up with her smile.

She said, "I'd love to. Yes."

• • •

Excited about my new love project in Effie, my daydreams were all about her. She danced behind my eyelids, her colourful hair trailing behind her. She smiled in my direction and I imagined our embrace.

There was a buzz on the intercom from downstairs. I was expecting no-one.

"Hello," I answered.

Front door sounds were heard echoing in the lobby hallway. Some distant voices. Somebody must have let the person in. It could have been a delivery person or just a wrong number. Having walked away from the intercom, I kept looking in the direction of the doorway. If anyone came up, they'd be up within a few minutes. I listened carefully and heard the elevator drive up without stopping.

I went back to sorting art supplies for my classes. Trying to conjure up Effie's face again, like when going back to sleep, re-dreaming the same scenario.

Then the knock came.

My heart jumped up to my neck. My cheeks flushed. I rushed to the door as if Effie read my mind on the other side. I didn't even check the peephole. My desires were so assured.

The door was wide open now.

He was still wearing that t-shirt, with my artwork on it.

There was something else too. By his waist, he gripped a silver handgun. Pointed at me.

Like a cannonball, close range, to the gut.

I heard the shot.

I felt the force.

And that's the last thing I remember.